PUBLIC SPEAKING

Public Speaking Guide on How to Talk to Anyone by Improving Social Intelligence Skills & Build Persuasive Relationship

(Effortless Conversations and Workplace Talk Done Right)

Dan Weissman

Published by Rob Miles

© **Dan Weissman**

All Rights Reserved

Charisma: Public Speaking Guide on How to Talk to Anyone by Improving Social Intelligence Skills & Build Persuasive Relationship (Effortless Conversations and Workplace Talk Done Right)

ISBN 978-1-989990-08-7

All rights reserved. No part of this guide may be reproduced in any form without permission in writing from the publisher except in the case of brief quotations embodied in critical articles or reviews.

Legal & Disclaimer

The information contained in this book is not designed to replace or take the place of any form of medicine or professional medical advice. The information in this book has been provided for educational and entertainment purposes only.

The information contained in this book has been compiled from sources deemed reliable, and it is accurate to the best of the Author's knowledge; however, the Author cannot guarantee its accuracy and validity and cannot be held liable for any errors or omissions. Changes are periodically made to this book. You must consult your doctor or get professional medical advice before using any of the suggested remedies, techniques, or information in this book.

Upon using the information contained in this book, you agree to hold harmless the Author from and against any damages, costs, and expenses, including any legal fees potentially resulting from the application of any of the information provided by this guide. This disclaimer applies to any damages or injury caused by the use and application, whether directly or indirectly, of any advice or information presented, whether for breach of contract, tort, negligence, personal injury, criminal intent, or under any other cause of action.

You agree to accept all risks of using the information presented inside this book. You need to consult a professional medical practitioner in order to ensure you are both able and healthy enough to participate in this program.

Table of Contents

INTRODUCTION 1

CHAPTER 1 WHY YOU SHOULD BE A SPEAKER 2

CHAPTER 2: ESSENTIAL NON-VERBAL COMMUNICATION WHEN DELIVERING A SPEECH. 13

CHAPTER 3: LET'S GET TO WORK 23

CHAPTER 4: SPEECH DELIVERY 32

CHAPTER 5: HONESTY: BE HONEST WITH YOURSELF 57

CHAPTER 6: OVER-SIMPLIFY YOUR WORD CHOICE 67

CHAPTER 7: THE FEAR FACTOR 70

CHAPTER 8:FOREPLAY 78

CHAPTER 9: GREAT IDEAS FOR OPENINGS IN YOUR SPEECH 86

CHAPTER 10: CONSIDER THE PURPOSE OF YOUR PRESENTATION 89

CHAPTER 11: BODY LANGUAGE TECHNIQUES FOR PUBLIC SPEAKING 97

CHAPTER 12: CONTEXTS OF PUBLIC SPEAKING 100

CHAPTER 13: WE ALL HAVE TO GO ON THE STAGE 106

CHAPTER 14: I SEE OVER 80% OF SPEAKERS MAKE THESE TWO MISTAKES 111

CHAPTER 15: DEALING WITH GLOSSOPHOBIA OR THE FEAR OF PUBLIC SPEAKING 121

CHAPTER 16: USE YOUR "CRUTCHES" 133

CHAPTER 17: WRITING YOUR MATERIAL 137

CHAPTER 18: GROUP COMMUNICATION JEOPARDY STYLEHEATHER PENN 161

CHAPTER 19: 15 TIPS THAT WILL HELP TRANSFORM YOU 167

CHAPTER 20: FURTHER PREPARATION 173

CHAPTER 21: HOW TO ORGANIZE AND ASSEMBLE YOUR PRESENTATION 179

CONCLUSION 191

Introduction

Public speaking is something that relatively few people ever have to do, which is a good thing since most people dread the very thought of it. Unfortunately, it is something that you might be required to do for your job, school or some other formal setting. The good news is that considerable research has been done to determine what makes public speaking such a stressful endeavor.

That research has revealed numerous ways to help a person improve their public speaking skills, as well as to reduce the stress and anxiety of public speaking itself. This book will reveal twenty different ways in which you can turn your greatest fear into your greatest triumph. By the time you finish this book, you will be ready, willing and able to handle any public speaking event with total calm and confidence, the true mark of a public speaking master!

Chapter 1
Why You Should Be A Speaker

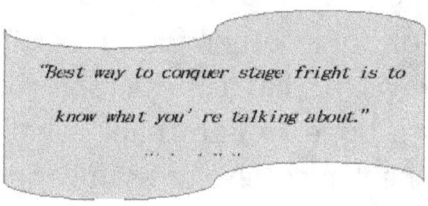

"Best way to conquer stage fright is to know what you're talking about."

Speaking gives you credibility as a leader or expert

Being a speaker is one of the fastest ways to build credibility as an expert. Sidenote: The other way is to having a book which is something else I teach on. Now back to speaking, the simple reason behind this is that if you are on the stage, you are in control of the environment. When you are in control of the environment and you are effective with it, you can control the activity within that environment.

When you think about it, if you are the speaker for the room that means you possibly know something more than everyone else that is there. You are able to give information to others and educate others. Everyone is listening to you and watching you. During the time in which you are speaking, if you are prepared, you can determine the outcome of your situation by the words that you use.

The people who make the best incomes are those who are able to command the room. I won't sit here and say that they are the smartest in the room. However, they have learned the skillset to command the room and be seen as the expert. This only happens with preparation and repetition.

For me, the way I started off building my own credibility was small. I did smaller events until the day I was able to command a room of more than 10,000 people. However, what I said in front of a room of 5 was not much different than what I said in front of those 10,000. The only thing different was the number of times I had done it. The more I spoke, the more credibility I built. One thing I know for sure is that if you don't start, it can't happen.

Public Speakers advance faster in their careers

This also aligns with building credibility. It's thought that the person who is able to command the room is the most knowledgeable, so with that said, it also helps you with better advancement.

Many people believe that when I talk about public speaking I am only referring to getting in front of a group of people to deliver some education, program, or opportunity. However, there are many executives who have to prepare talks for work. Their talks determine if they rise in their career or not.

Let me just keep it all the way real with you. If you don't know how to effectively communicate, it is very difficult to actually build anything, whether it's a business or a career. Think about it, in everything we do we have to be able to be effective with our communication.

That's why if you work on perfecting your talks, you can most definitely advance faster in your career. From management positions where you have to be able to motivate your staff to top sales professionals who have to inspire their clients to take action, speaking is much bigger than just a stage in front of hundreds or thousands. Some of the biggest checks are made right in the board rooms. It's definitely very valuable to become skilled in your industry or career and learn how to be effective in communicating, so you can increase your check!

Public speaking helps you connect with people... if you do it with empathy!

Have you ever heard the saying that, "People don't care how much you know until they know how much you care?" If you haven't, then this is a great opportunity for me to bring a bit of revelation to you. When you are a great speaker, you're able to connect with the crowd.

I have seen some incredible business men and women totally kill their careers and businesses because they don't learn this important factor when it comes to speaking in front of people. Remember, when you are speaking in front of people, these people all have life going on. They are thinking about several other things while you are speaking. However, when you are able to become empathetic in a way that allows your audience to identify with you, it's a most amazing feeling because you are able to connect with them on a more intimate level. One of the most incredible feelings is when you've finished a talk and someone comes up to you and tells you that your story or your talk has inspired them to move into action, or that it has changed their life.

Some of the most accomplished speakers in the world are best known for being able to connect with the audience regardless of the audience's background. When this is done, so much impact is made. When you become really good at connecting with people, your income will be substantial. You will have other organizations seeking you out because they want you to impact their network as well. There is no better feeling than being able to connect with other people. Before we move on to the steps of being a great speaker, one piece of advice I will give is that in order to connect with your audience, you must also take time to know your audience. Knowing your audience will help you tremendously.

Public Speaking can be very profitable

Public speaking can become extremely profitable when you learn how to develop the craft of speaking and communication.

The main goal is to first identify what your goal is as a speaker. Are you looking to sell products or services? Do you want to get paid to be a keynote speaker? You have to identify what kind of speaker you want to be. I'll actually discuss the different kinds of speakers in Chapter 2.

According to Sokanu.com, a career matching platform, the average income for a public speaker's earnings in the United States is determined by seniority. If you are not familiar with seniority, I am meaning the number of years this person has been speaking as well as how many people they've spoken in front of. This does not include what you can make internationally. Also, keep in mind this is more so for the person who wants to get a check as a speaker versus someone who is selling products and services.

Top end public speaker earnings are recorded with the highest earnings at $49.64 an hour, $103,240 per year. Senior public speaker earnings average $36.14 an hour, $75,180 per year. Experienced public speaker earnings come in at $26.41 an hour or $54,940 per year. Junior public speaker earnings are $19.37 an hour, $40,290 per year. Starting public speaker earnings are just $14.80 an hour or $30,790 per year. If you truly become an effective communicator, you can grow your income tremendously.

Personally, I started my professional speaking in the industry of network marketing, also known as multi-level marketing. This is one of those industries where you invite people to come to your home or a hotel and share with them an opportunity to make money from home in a home-based business.

I was in two different companies before I transitioned over to doing my own workshops. However, in both of those companies, I was able to make multiple six figures per year. It wasn't because I was the smartest. It wasn't because I did more meetings (even though I did a lot). I wasn't because I prospected more people. The reason why I was so successful was because I was effective with communication and connecting with people. I was able to become part of the top 1% of income earners in the industry because I was effective in communication.

If you are in network marketing and you are reading this book, pay close attention to the top income earners in your company. Nine times out of 10 they are really good on the stage. It takes practice, but with practice you can earn six figures or even millions as a speaker.

Develops confidence

It may come to you as a surprise that speaking in public builds confidence. The reason I say this is because most people are deathly afraid to speak in public. If you have a fear of public speaking, don't worry! I have you covered in another chapter, but right now let's focus on this. Yes, it's so true that the more you speak the better you get, and the more confident you become.

Before I started doing workshops and trainings, I was extremely shy. I sometimes still find myself falling back into that shy place after speaking in front of a crowd. Just like speaking gives you credibility with others, it also gives you the feeling of credibility within. When you are effective with your communication, you can feel the energy of the room and the energy become contagious. It will help bring in an excitement that one can only know when they are in that moment. I don't even know how to explain it other than to say that you must try it.

Trust me, it will be scary at first, but when you continue to do more and more, and you develop a talk that you know like you know the back of your hand, your confidence will radiate throughout the room. When you are confident, others feel it as well, and they become confident. Keep in mind that this confidence only grows as you practice your talk and develop your skills in communicating.

Makes you more promotable

When you're given the title of being a public speaker, no matter what type of speaker you are, it most definitely makes you more promotable. The reason this is the case is that when you think about it, as a speaker you are doing what most never would. Speaking in public is a top fear. In the eyes of many, if you have this title, it makes you more attractive in the market place.

As a speaker, you stand out from everyone else. You make it easier for a person to promote your products or services because if they bring you in as a speaker, you can do that part for them. It's all together a great title for you to have as a professional and will help you to increase your value in the marketplace.

Chapter 2: Essential Non-Verbal Communication When Delivering A Speech.

Your voice is very important when speaking and it is all that an audience has when listening to you on the radio. (See the section on 'speaking on the radio').

Usually, however, the speaker is visible to the audience either 'in the flesh' in a hall or meeting room or visible via television or video-conference.

What the audience sees is as important as what it hears.

Your physical appearance is important.

When you stand up to speak, all eyes are on you. Many in your audience will make up their mind about you, rather than your speech, in the first few seconds - whatever you say. In fact, they might already have done so when they are made aware of you when introduced by the chairman or you come on stage.

You must be neat

As those who know me will confirm, I am not naturally a neat person. I have been guilty of all of the following mistakes when speaking in public:

· Forgetting to comb my hair.

· Wearing socks that are not appropriate.

· Wearing socks that do not match.

· Forgetting to straighten my tie.

· Having my shirt-tail hanging out.

· Having my trouser belt hanging loose.

· Forgetting to change the trainers I wore while driving to the venue for the well-polished formal shoes I was supposed to wear.

· Not tying up my shoelaces properly.

I hope that you will avoid the above or similar mistakes as audiences do notice - and sometimes comment.

Your clothes must suit the occasion.

For a man the safest bet is a suit. It is better to be too formal rather than 'improperly' dressed. Women have slightly more freedom, but remember that people such as Angela Merkel, get away with various sorts of blazer type jackets in order to ring the changes. Dark colours are not required at all times.

However, being a man, I have worn a dark suit when being interviewed, inspecting schools or participating in church functions. I have worn a suit but in a 'non-threatening' colour such as dark blue or dark green when training teachers. I have worn 'smart informal' clothes when meeting colleagues, with or without a tie. (I am one of the generation that normally wears a tie). I have also worn a pullover and trousers when speaking informally to groups of friends.

If I were a travel representative welcoming new guests to a hotel on the Costa Brava, it might be appropriate to wear a flowery shirt, shorts and sandals. If the hotel manager greets guests I would, however, expect him to be more formally dressed.

If you are not sure – check with your organiser. You do not want to be the only one not wearing a suit if everybody else is. You do not want to find yourself wearing a formal suit when everybody else, including the chairman, is in jeans and a pullover.

Your stance and elimination of any physical barriers to communicating with your audience

Generally we stand up when we speak in public. The way we get up and the way we stand says a lot about us.

When we are confident we stand up straight, we face the audience and move our eyes and bodies to 'take in' the whole of the audience. We also indicate by our gestures that 'we are all in this together'. If we do not face the audience directly, huddle our shoulders and use no gestures when we speak, we will appear to be unfriendly, disinterested or indeed nervous.

Although we might be using a lectern or table, we do not hide behind it. Very often we move our body's position to face various sections of the audience and to emphasise our message.

If you are in a position to arrange things, you want the minimum of physical barriers between yourself and your audience (safety and security permitting).

You are not going to interact properly with your audience if the caretaker of a school hall has placed a table on a stage and expects you to address the parents, governors or teachers from there.

In the past I have brought the table down from the stage. It is still useful as it allows colleagues to take minutes or to sit for a question and answer session. A table can also hold documents. I have, however, stood in front of the table when I have talked to the audience. I have also talked from the side of a lectern when I no longer need the notes the lectern holds.

Your facial expressions and gestures must be natural and come from the heart, so that you project yourself to the audience

Both of these are vital when creating empathy with your audience.

Even though your face might appear to be very small to spectators when you stand in front of a large audience, those present will be fully aware of your expressions. From a very early age, humans are conditioned to examine faces to judge the mood and feelings of others.

There is no point in rehearsing expressions or gestures in front of a mirror because others know if your expressions are artificial or rehearsed.

Your eyes will tell your audience a lot. If you smile, your eyes need to smile as well. Your eyes will show whether you are genuinely interested in what you are saying or whether it is an act.

You may well change your expression to match the mood of what you are saying without consciously knowing it. I say this because if you practise expressions they will probably look contrived. As you deliver your speech:

· You may laugh rather than smile

· You might stop smiling if you have a sombre or serious message.

· You might well frown if there is something of which you disapprove

· Your eyes might sparkle with enthusiasm or love

· Your eyes might darken with anger.

· Your brows might be furrowed with anxiety.

Gestures are also important.

Perhaps politicians do practice wide sweeps of the arms - they might well do so, but people know if gestures are artificial.

The use of gestures will vary from one individual to another, from one culture to another. Generally they are used sparingly and only in support of what is being said.

Gestures might be somewhat restricted if you are holding a microphone in one hand but they are still used.

It would be impossible to describe all gestures and what they are meant to represent but again, as humans, we seem to have a common understanding of what the gestures mean. If you were to watch a politician speaking on television with the volume turned down, you would not hear the words but you could judge his or her mood, urgency and so on from his or her gestures.

Here are some gestures and their probable social and emotional meaning.

· Hands outstretched with 'enclosing hands' -"My fellows, we are all in this together."

· Finger over the mouth - "This is a secret" or "be quiet".

· Finger pointing – "indicating something we should look at."

- Clenched fist – "determination, threat of violence".
- Hands outstretched with palms up – "I have nothing to hide".
- A shrug of the shoulders "I don't know", "I don't care"
- Hand near ear- "listen carefully".
- Hand with finger pointing to the eye – "watch".
- Arms/ hands moving up and down "I want to emphasise this"
- One outstretched arm held high (like some kinds of salute) –" a call to arms"
- Beating the lectern or the other hand with a fist. "I am very angry".

Some gestures are culturally significant- such as Kruschev taking off his shoe and striking the table with it. This showed his anger. Some of the gestures above will have different connotations in different cultures.

Make no mistake, speeches can have strong emotional effects and the effect the orator wants to create is often greatly enhanced by gesture and facial expression.

Chapter 3: Let's Get To Work

I. SPEECH FORMAT

Here is a simple format that you can follow to write your speech. Just fill it out and that's it, no more, no less!

A. INTRODUCTION

Usually written in one paragraph only, this first part of the speech aims to arouse the attention of the audience, present the main idea (or thesis) and the purpose of the speech, and give an overview of the main points of the speech. The following parts compose the introduction:

1. Hook: This is a statement that grabs the audience's attention. It intrigues, draws in, and motivates the audience to keep on listening to the speech. Some commonly used attention-grabbing techniques are the following:

Telling an anecdote

Citing a quotation

Asking rhetorical or thought-provoking questions

Sharing some background information

Giving a riddle or puzzle

2. Thesis statement: This is a sentence that states the central idea of the speech.

3. Purpose: This reveals the goal of the speech. It explains how the audience can benefit from listening to the speech.

4. Overview of the main points: this provides the audience a brief overview of the main points that the speech will tackle. It gives the audience an idea of the flow of the speech.

B. BODY

Following the introduction is the body of the speech. The body explains, develops, and supports the thesis statement using details, evidence (e.g., statistics, testimony), and examples. It is typically composed of three paragraphs.

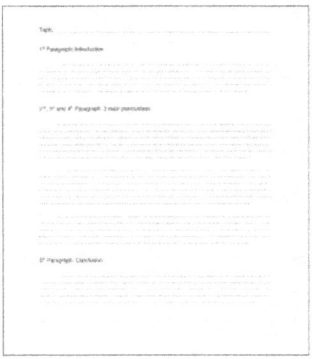

Each paragraph has a topic sentence (or the main idea of the paragraph) and several supporting sentences. To link one paragraph to the next, transitions are used.

These are words or phrases that show relationships between ideas and ensure a smooth flow from one point to the next. Here are some examples of transitions:

To add an idea: in addition, moreover, further, also

To show similarity: similarly, likewise, in the same way, in like manner

To contrast: on the other hand, however, but, on the contrary

To illustrate: for example, specifically, in particular, notably

To emphasize: more importantly, above all, indeed, in fact

C. CONCLUSION

This is the last part of the speech. The conclusion reiterates the thesis statement and summarizes the main points covered in the body of the speech. It also contains a final, memorable statement (e.g., quote, metaphor, advice, challenge or call to action) that provides closure or helps the audience remember the speech.

II. HOW TO MEMORIZE YOUR SPEECH?

Do you have a good memory? How do you usually memorize something, say, a paragraph? What do you do when you forget some of the lines?

A speaker gives a memorized speech by committing every word of the speech to memory and then delivering it in front of an audience.

The speaker does not bring with him or her any notes or manuscript.

Unless you are an exceptionally proficient speaker, speaking from memory is usually appropriate for relatively short speeches such as when presenting or accepting an award, making an announcement, giving an opening or closing remarks, or introducing a speaker.

After writing your speech, these are the steps you need to follow.

Step 1: Read your speech several times and understand it

During this time, just read your speech several times without worrying how you deliver it. Read in the morning, at noon and in the evening.

READ IT TWO TIMES A DAY FOR 3 DAYS. Do this in the morning and in the evening. Don't memorize, just read and get familiar with it.

Step 2: Memorize by paragraph

By this time, you are familiar with your speech. It's time to get serious and focus on the main ideas of your speech.

MEMORIZE BY PARAGRAPH.

On the 4th DAY, memorize the 1st paragraph or the greetings and introduction.

Do it seriously and stay away from distractions like TV, mobile phone, computer and others that could divert your attention.

Do this for the whole day and nothing more.

On the 5th day, memorize the second paragraph, keeping close attention on the three main ideas.

Do this for the whole day and nothing more.

On the 6th day, memorize the third and final paragraph giving close attention to the summary and closing.

Do this for the whole day and nothing more.

On the 7th day, you are already familiar with the whole speech.

Review each paragraph and go over the whole script of your speech.

Now, you are ready to proceed, it's time to practice.

Step 3: Practice, practice, practice!

The mirror is your best friend.

The next thing to do is to PRACTICE YOUR SPEECH IN FRONT OF THE MIRROR or anywhere you are comfortable.

Avoid practices in your bedroom; the temptation of lying down is huge and it is not good for you.

Too much comfort could disrupt your attention and focus. Stay away from your bed.

Chapter 4: Speech Delivery

Learning public speaking is like baking a cake! Once you have the appropriate baking equipment (mindset), selected the right recipe (message), added all the cake ingredients (key points within the speech), baked it (practiced the speech) the cake is ready to be iced - delivery of the speech!

To become an engaging and captivating speaker your delivery techniques and style need to be developed and honed. However, whilst your audience will appreciate dynamic delivery - warning - don't over cook it! Many speakers fall into the trap of only focusing on delivery. The audience may be engaged but if the speech structure is not clear, the overarching message is missing and your mindset is not healthy you run a risk. You run the risk that the delivery becomes like a cake that looks really appealing but when you actually have a slice it is disappointing.

With that warning in mind, investing in your delivery is important and can really add to the overall quality of your speech and bring your speech content alive. The delivery stage is comprised of three key components: your voice, eye contact and body language. In this section we share the following tips:

First is **How to have a captivating voice.** Your voice is crucial in public speaking as it is the delivery tool used to share your message. In this section we share tips designed to help ensure your voice has maximum impact.

Second is **How to have engaging eye contact.** One of the best ways to build rapport with your audience is to actually look at them. In this section we share tips which will ensure your eye contact makes your audience feel noticed and valued.

Thirds is **How to use your body language effectively.** Your hands, feet, arms and legs may normally be very easy to keep under control. However, standing in front of audience with nerves pumping through your veins your body can do crazy and unexpected things. In this section we share ways you can use your body language to add and not detract from your speech.

SECTION 1

HOW TO HAVE A CAPTIVATING VOICE

"The human voice is the most beautiful instrument of all,

but it is the most difficult to play"

~ Richard Strauss

In public speaking, your voice is crucial as it is the delivery tool used to share your message. In this section we share with you eight tips designed to help ensure your voice has maximum impact.

1. HARNESS THE POWER OF THE PAUSE

A pause is a gap you deliberately add between points or before punchlines. When pauses are well timed and executed, they can have many benefits including:

Firstly, they help the audience absorb information more easily. The audience processes information when you are silent not when you are talking. Even pausing for a fraction of a second between points can make a speech much easier to understand.

Secondly, they give power to punchlines. A well timed pause before or after a punchline can charge your delivery making the punchline much more powerful and effective.

Thirdly, pauses can help declutter sentences ensuring you only use your voice to deliver words of meaning and value. For example, pauses can help to eradicate filler words such as um, ah, so, you know - the list goes on!

Finally, pausing during your speech is like a mini break for your voice which helps in avoiding dips in the quality of your voice. This becomes very important particularly when delivering longer speeches.

2. TAKE A DEEP BREATH

Before leaping into the speaking space it is recommended to take a few deep breaths. This helps your voice in two key ways:

Firstly, if you are really nervous, your voice can be shaky making it harder to articulate. Taking a few deep breaths can help bring your nerves under control and give your voice stability.

Secondly, taking deep breaths can prevent you from getting breathless when speaking. Often when speakers don't have enough air in their lungs their volume can dip especially at the end of long sentences. A few deep breaths before starting to speak can enhance the quality of your voice and help get your nerves under control.

3. EMBRACE THE SOUND OF YOUR OWN VOICE

Too many people cringe at the sound of their own voice. Imagine if a drummer despised the drum, it would be tricky to be a top quality musician. As a speaker your voice is your instrument which you need to be able to work with and fine tune. One way to start training your ear is to listen to your voicemail instead of avoiding it. As a public speaker you need to learn to at least accept the sound of your own voice. Note aspects of your voice which you like and areas that you might want to improve on but most of all make a commitment to embracing the sound of your own voice.

4. STAY HYDRATED - DRINK WATER

Dehydration is something that you want to avoid as a public speaker. Many speakers forget to drink before a speech or they worry that they will need the bathroom whilst delivering so they don't drink for hours before stepping on stage.

Dehydration has a number of impacts. It can cause your energy levels to drop making your voice more flat and less engaging. If you are using a microphone it can lead to a repetitive ticking sound which can be irritating for your audience. Dehydration also causes dry mouth which can impact on the quality of your voice. The best way to stay hydrated is to drink water. You can even take a bottle on stage especially when speaking for a longer time. It can be a natural way of taking a pause provided you don't draw unnecessary attention to the fact that you are taking a drink.

5. PUMP UP THE VOLUME

As children when we are first learning to talk we are encouraged to speak up but as we go through childhood and school we are encouraged to keep the volume down or shut up altogether. No wonder by adulthood we are confused as to what the optimum volume level is. It is vital when public speaking that you can be heard. Most speakers in the absence of a microphone tend to lack volume. When we have the optimum volume not only does it break down barriers in engaging with the audience and holding their attention but it can also add to your authority and stage presence. When projecting your voice many speakers feel like they are shouting when they are not. It is recommended you aim your conversational volume level by speaking to those at the back of the room as opposed to the front, that way everyone in the room will be able to hear you. If using a microphone remember all you need to do is speak normally. There is no need to shout as the volume can be adjusted accordingly. It is vital that you can be heard and as a speaker it is your responsibility to pump up the volume accordingly.

6. BE INTENTIONAL ABOUT PACE

For many speakers they have one objective in mind when they get on stage - to get off as fast as possible. One way this comes across to the audience is in the pace of speech.

Some speakers appear like they are aiming for a Guinness world record based on the number of words they can pump out per minute. This has a number of downfalls including:

It can make a presentation very challenging to keep up with. Remember, the audience has very low attention spans and can get overwhelmed with ideas very easily. By slowing down you give them time to think and process information.

It can impact your voice - your volume may go down as your voice gets tired, your words may start to run together, articulation of individual words may be poor and you may get breathless due to lack of pausing. Speaking in this way puts undue pressure on your voice and can make you feel exhausted.

For any speaker, the ultimate goal with pace is to learn to vary it to ensure momentum. In some parts you speed up in others slow down. The contrast in speed will add to your delivery and help to hold the attention of the audience.

7. INJECT INTONATION FOR INTEREST

Intonation is the change of the pitch of your voice. The best story tellers are very aware of the importance of intonation. Their secret ingredient is not only great content, but also engaging intonation.

Some speakers have natural intonation - the pitch of their voice goes up and down making it interesting and captivating, while others have flat voices making it difficult for the audience to listen to regardless of how interesting the content of their speeches is.

If your voice tends to be flat it does not mean that you can't practice intonation. Developing intonation in your voice is a skill like any other. If you want to have an interesting voice you need to be intentional about it. One way to do this is to go through your speech and highlight certain phrases and words that you want to emphasise with your voice and then practice saying them at different pitches till you get it right.

8. KEEP A SMILEY BRIGHT FACE

Having energy on stage as a speaker is so important and one of the key ways to achieve this is to have energy in your voice. Having energy is your voice is a combination of many aspects including volume, pace, intonation and adding in a smile. A smile not only brightens up your face making it easier to build rapport with the audience but it also makes your voice sound more friendly and energetic. You don't want to have a weird, unnatural, fake smile on stage, but a natural smile goes a long way and it brings energy into your voice which can change the atmosphere.

SECTION 2

HOW TO HAVE AN ENGAGING EYE CONTACT

"Eye contact is way more intimate

than words will ever be"

~ Faraaz Kazi

With so much time now spent staring at a computer screen or a smart phone, looking into the eyes of other people is probably even more confronting than ever before. Making eye contact in public speaking is essential in building rapport with your audience. Below are 5 tips to assist you in having effective eye contact with your audience:

1. LOOK AT THE AUDIENCE

Many speakers pluck up their courage to get on stage but nerves and perhaps intimidation can prevent them from looking into the eyes of the audience members. It is common to avoid eye contact at all costs and here are some typical pitfalls:

Firstly, making more eye contact with the floor than the audience. Not trying to pick on them, but university lecturers are often guilty of this! It can appear like they have their lecture notes stuck to the floor instead of ingrained in their brain. As a speaker, if you stare intently at the floor you miss the opportunity to engage with your audience.

Secondly, looking at the ceiling. This may plant doubt in the minds of your audience about whether you know what you are talking about. They may think you are trying to recall information, or it may even give the impression you think you're better than your audience and that you enjoy looking right over them.

Thirdly, staring out the window or the door. It gives the impression you are planning an escape route and that anything going on around about you is more exciting than speaking to them.

Finally staring at your notes and/or PowerPoint. This may cause the audience to think you don't know your topic and you are very nervous even if this is not the case!

Be aware therefore of these pitfalls and be sure to actually look your audience in the eyes. One way to help you do this is to see the audience as individuals and not as an army about to destroy you!

2. EVENLY DISTRIBUTE EYE CONTACT

Sometimes when standing on stage it can feel like you are trapped on a deserted island. On a deserted island, you scan the horizon wishing, waiting, hoping for a rescue boat or plane. It can be very similar on stage. You look out into the sea of faces looking for help in the audience and there they are: a smiling, happy and nodding face! You lock eyes with them and it is like no one else in the room exists. You present all your thoughts and ideas to them and it makes you feel great! Only two problems - what about the rest of the audience? and what about the person you locked eyes with? The rest of the audience will feel disconnected and unengaged. And the person you locked us with may feel very uncomfortable!

It is important with eye contact to ensure that you aim to engage with everyone equally and not favour one side of the room or one single person.

3. ACKNOWLEDGE THE CHEAP SEATS

In most rooms there tends to be one or two of the audience that end up in the cheap seats. Restricted view because of the pillar, seated right at the side of the stage and worst of all sat at a round table with their back to the stage having to twist and strain to even see the stage. Sometimes having cheap seats in a room is totally out of your control as a speaker. To remedy the situation be intentional about making eye contact with these individuals. This will go along way in making them feel comfortable and a valued member of the audience.

4. ADJUST TO THE AUDIENCE SIZE

Just as our eyes adjust focus for short distances compared to long distances, so too should our eye contact adjust depending on the size of the audience. As a speaker your eye contact strategy should be different for an audience of 20 compared to say an audience of 200. For an audience of 20 you would want to make eye contact with each audience member for a few seconds at a time and perhaps multiple times depending on the duration of the speech. For 200, it won't be possible to make eye contact with each individual. In this case it is recommend to split the room into a number of sections and focus on each section at a time making eye contact with individuals in each section without favouring a particular section or individual. That way everyone in the room is more likely to be engaged and feel like you have acknowledged them.

5. AVOID MENTAL TRICKS

Over the years there have been many tips about eye contact - look just above the tops of the audience's heads and not their faces, or, even more interesting the notion of imaging your audience naked! There are a number of drawbacks to both of these.

Firstly, if you look at the top of their heads as a speaker you're the one missing out. The facial expressions of audience members can be a very effective indicator of how engaged they are. You miss the chance to make small tweaks to your speech as you go by doing this. Also, eye contact is about building connection, it is not about tricking the audience into thinking that you are looking into their eyes.

Secondly, imagining the audience naked could lead to all kinds of unhelpful facial expressions that you as the speaker may be unaware of. What if your highly physically attractive or unattractive boss is in the audience, what is the plan then? It is also another trick that leads to losing that genuine connection with the audience.

It is recommended not to adopt any tricks to avoid making real, genuine eye contact with your audience.

SECTION 3

HOW TO USE BODY LANGUAGE EFFECTIVELY

"Language is a more recent technology.

Your body language, your eyes, your energy

will come through to the audience even

before you start speaking"

~ Peter Guber

Your hands, feet, arms and legs may normally be very easy to keep under control. However, in front of an audience with nerves pumping through your veins and your mind concentrated on recalling content, your body can do crazy and unexpected things. In this section we share ways you can use your body language to add and not detract from your speech.

1. TAKE CENTRE STAGE

Your body talks and hence we refer to it as body language. As a speaker where you choose to position yourself on stage says a lot about you without having to say a single word. Many speakers lurk at the back or sides of the stage. Other speakers take centre stage but then stand at an angle to the audience. Hiding at the back or sides of the stage can make engaging with the audience more challenging and suggests to the audience that you are a nervous speaker. Standing at an angle on stage can really impact your ability to equally distribute eye contacting with your audience as more likely than not you will favour the part of the audience your body is angled towards. Taking centre stage and being square on to your audience speaks volumes. It says I am in control, I have command and I have authority without having to say a word. It adds power to your delivery.

2. KEEP FEET PLANTED

For some speakers nerves manifest in their feet. The rest of their body appears calm and under control but their feet tell a different story. Common tell tale signs of nerves include constant redistribution of weight from foot to foot, the shoe shuffle and more pronounced movement that could look like contemporary dance. As a speaker you don't want anything to distract the audience. Therefore if you are standing still it is recommended to plant your feet. Doing this will not only avoid common issues with feet but similar to taking centre stage it lets your audience know your cool, calm and in control.

3. KEEP LEGS STILL

Sometimes when standing up to speak your legs respond in unhelpful ways. This can include standing cross legged which can affect balance and can cause the audience to wonder if the speaker needs the bathroom. It maybe that your legs shake making it challenging to retain composure. Or most dramatically your legs could go from underneath you causing you to fall over. To ensure you are stable, it is recommended to aim to keep your legs still whilst standing stationary.

4. MAINTAIN NATURAL HAND GESTURES

On our training courses we often get asked what should I do with my hands? Our advice is to aim to keep your arms and hands loosely by your side and be natural. If your hands normally move when you talk then go for it but just be mindful of what you are doing with them. You want to avoid a number of motions: aeroplane arms, aggressively pointing, clapping, giving yourself a hand massage, folding your arms or fidgeting (itching/scratching/tugging at your hair/clothes). You can use your hands to complement the speech structure such as counting your key points out using your fingers. Or you can raise your arm to indicate to the audience that you want a show of hands in response to a question. Whatever you do purposefully with your arms and hands the golden rule is be natural. This will help you to build a genuine connection and rapport with your audience.

5. MAINTAIN STRONG FRAME

Some speakers stand or sit on stage slumped over, with rounded shoulders and with their head hung low. This may signal to the audience a lack of self confidence. It is therefore recommended that you do your best to stand/sit on stage with your shoulders back, chin up, posture as straight as possible and with your head up. This helps your delivery by indicating you are confident, helps to ensure your eyes don't wander about the floor and enhances your stage presence.

6. MOVE WITH PURPOSE

If you want to move on stage then make sure you move with purpose. You want to be like an experienced hillwalker who has a goal as opposed to a wandering soul out for a stroll mapless and lost. If you move aimlessly on stage then it can be more distracting than standing still. In a similar vein marching repeatedly from one side of the stage to the other can make the audience feel like they have been catapulted into a tennis match. It is therefore recommended that you aim to move with purpose on stage. What is meant by this? It means aligning your movement on stage with your speech. If for example you are sharing an idea with two opposing view you may consider moving to one side of the stage when sharing one view and the other side of the stage for the other. It not only means you are using the stage but it actually helps your audience to see that you have changed perspectives in not only what you're saying but also in your body language. In a similar way you could consider moving on stage as you move from one key point to the next, Similar to the previous example this lets your audience know you are finished with one point and have quite literally moved onto another. Remember if you are going to move, make sure you move for a purpose.

7. WEAR COMFORTABLE ATTIRE

For many speakers fidgeting and tugging on your clothes, accessories such as jewelery or a tie or even hair is common. This can be one of the most distracting forms of body language for the audience. Just like a pair of bright coloured socks says something about your personality, fidgeting and tugging at your clothes suggests as a speaker you are uncomfortable and nervous. Comfortable attire does not mean sweat pants and running shoes - it is obviously very important to wear appropriate clothing given the nature, location, type of event and the audience. However in selecting appropriate attire it is important to wear something you feel good in, comfortable and confident. Wear your favorite power suit, your killer heels or your bright patterned tie - whatever works for you within reason! If you are comfortable in your clothes there's far more chance you will have open body language, not feel the need to fidget and appear relaxed on stage.

8. DEVELOP AN ENGAGING FACIAL EXPRESSION

When we think body language we tend to think hands, feet, legs and arms and we tend to forget about facial expressions. However, facial expressions are really important and powerful in not only building rapport with the audience but in the quality of your body language. You can be saying all the right things but if your facial expressions are contrary to the message it can have a very negative impact on how your body language is perceived by the audience. Many speakers either look blank, very serious or probably the worst - angry! To ensure your body language is aligned head to toe be aware of your facial expressions particularly when you know you tend to be very animated. Aim to look friendly and most important be determined to make the most of your time on stage and let the enjoyment reflect on your face!

Chapter 5: Honesty: Be Honest With Yourself

The secret to being a very good public speaker is to ensure that you are always honest with yourself. It is close to impossible for you to be able to speak powerfully if you cannot be truthful with yourself.

Think about this; you are supposed to give a speech about a new program that your company has just launched, and you are supposed to tell your audience how awesome, how effective the program is, but in real sense you know that the program is flawed and you do not like it one it. In such a case, you might be able to deliver a speech based on the speech notes that you have been given, but in the real sense you will struggle with delivering the speech convincingly.

There are some people who can be able to pull off such theatrics with their speeches, but let's be honest, not so many of us are able to lie about a lot of things, especially when you are delivering the speech to a huge audience. Trying to pretend that you do not feel what you really are feeling is an easy lead-up to what psychologists refer to as cognitive dissonance. This is a situation where you end up standing up for two views that are directly opposing one another at the same time, and before long, you will start contradicting yourself. Such a situation can become worse when the audience is already split along hating and loving the program, and in this case, the ones who hate the program can through their responses, will end up influencing your ability to give a good speech in the long run.

When you are honest with what you feel, it becomes easier for you to deliver a really good speech. It is like making peace with the demons in your head. You know they are there, and you know how to keep them at ease. However, if you cannot do this, things can turn from bad to worse in a very short time.

While delivering a speech, always remember that there are members of the audience that come prepared with some really tricky questions, and for this reason you have to be prepared for the worst, just in case things go south at any given time.

Besides, if you keep lying to yourself, you will have effectively managed to brainwash yourself before you even get to meet your audience, and with that you will have lost control of the audience, allowing them enough power to control you and the outcome of the speech.

Pay attention to the audience

There are three important elements of public speaking that will determine how effective you are when you are delivering your speech. These are:

The speech

The speaker

The audience

One of the standout qualities of a good public speaker is their ability to listen to the audience and respond appropriately. What most people do not know about public speaking is the fact that in as much as you are delivering the speech, you also need to be alert so that you can lend the audience a hearing.

Listening to the audience can be taken in different ways, either literally or in an implied manner. Literally speaking, you need to hear out your audience so that you can respond to their concerns, questions and anything else that they may raise during the speech. This is the simpler part because you are basically engaging with the audience based on the spoken word that they are sharing with you.

However, at the same time, a good public speaker needs to be able to pay attention to the implied messages that the audience is sending. These can be anything from gestures to facial and bodily expressions. The main reason why you need to understand these in particular is because the audience will in some cases not be able to outwardly face you and question a few things about your speech, but they will instead show their appreciation or disapproval of your speech through actions. This is especially so if there is a wide gap in superiority between your position in society and the position that the general audience enjoys.

Learning to listen to the audience will enable you learn beforehand how well they are taking to the speech, whether they are bored, or whether it is time for you to switch things up a gear. Rest assured that listening to the audience has everything to do with how successful you will be in delivering the speech.

In order to understand how important it is for you to pay attention to the needs of the audience, you can relate to a situation where someone tried to talk to you, and kept on talking for time on end without a care in the world about what your reaction is. It can be so frustrating because it feels like the interaction is one dimensional, while a good speech is supposed to be all-round, with all the participants involved in one way or the other.

One of the important things that you have to understand about public speaking is that it is not all about you who is delivering the speech, but it is also about the audience.

Now that we have stepped through many of the crucial tasks of have a great public speaking experience, it is easy to say, "now we are getting somewhere." You have a dynamite outline or script. You understand the audience, the venue and what you want to say. You know your material inside and out. Are you ready to go?

You are close to ready but there is a little more to do to prepare. A big step toward being ready to stand in front of that audience brimming with confidence is to practice your presentation. Even if that speech looks really good on paper, actually delivering it will surface any problems with the outline and it will give you the feel for what it is like to hear your own voice delivering that message.

Practicing your speech is especially important if you have not done a lot of public speaking because it helps you visualize what it will be like to give the speech. If you are working from an outline, you will experience that moment where you forget where you are in your plan and you can improve your outline so it is a safety net for you when you get in front of a crowd.

Brain Freeze

There is a common moment that almost every public speaker has that can be terrifying. It happens as you are speaking along and suddenly, your mind goes blank. The causes of this "brain freeze" can be several things. Stage fright can do it. You might have a small distraction like a sound outside the room or a sudden realization that your shirt is untucked. Something small like that is just enough to disrupt your concentration and put your mind into a locked condition.

Practicing your presentation gives you a chance to simulate that moment and learn how to get past it. You can be sure that you have seen experienced public speakers go through brain freeze but they are so smooth that they get themselves back on track and the audience never knows it. Part of that smooth confidence comes because that speaker knows his material and practiced that presentation so that his training kicked in and pulled him through the crisis.

How to Practice

There are several ways you can "test drive" your presentation. Of course, you can speak it into the mirror or simply read it out loud to yourself. This is not 100% effective because you will not try to project the ideas onto an audience when that audience is you.

A great way to practice your presentation is to gather some friends, associates or loved ones around and give the speech to them. Be sure they know how to behave like a real audience. If the talk is being given without interaction, make sure none is offered as you practice.

Give the speech to your test audience in conditions as close to how it will be when you deliver it live. If you will be standing up, stand up. If you will use a podium to work with your notes, create one and work with them. This exercise is about more than hearing your voice say the words. It is also about testing your notes and any other public speaking accessories that you need to work on that important day when you stand up to tell that audience what you want them to hear.

Another great idea is to have yourself filmed as you practice your speech so you can watch how you look and criticize your own performance. Let your friends and family offer constructive advice on how to make your delivery better. Then each time you make improvements, practice it again. There is one simple rule that is the law of the land during this phase of your presentation and this rule will turn you from a nervous public speaker into a confident one. That rule is "practice, practice, practice."

Chapter 6: Over-Simplify Your Word Choice

The last chapter, we talked about the three main verbal issues that can detract away from your presentation's message. Now, we're going to talk about the other big verbal issue that can impact your presentation: word choice.

During presentations, we tend to get much more verbose. We use bigger and more complex words in an attempt to sound more impressive. It's natural human nature.

This is absolutely not the way to go about doing so.

Your goal when presenting is to communicate a message to your audience. An audience will have a complete spectrum of people within it. On the one hand, there could be people in the audience who would understand and appreciate complicated vocabulary. On the other hand, there could be people who much prefer simple vocabulary.

Your goal here should be to go as broad as possible. You want to present language that everyone in the audience would understand and appreciate. While only some will understand the verbosity, everyone will understand the simple language.

Think about it this way: audiences are distracted. If someone looks down at their phone to read a text, then looks back up 30 seconds later to hear complicated vocabulary, they will be lost. If they look back up and hear simple language, it's easier for them to catch back up.

Therefore, I always use the five-year-old test. In other words, ask yourself: "would a five-year-old understand what I'm saying here?"

If the answer is yes, then great! The entire audience will be able to follow along. If not, make sure to change your language to simplify!

Another great check is the ten slides or less rule. Many presenters tend to over-index on material and create a large number of slides. The more slides you have, the higher the odds are the audience won't be able to follow along.

Stick to ten slides or less in your presentation that you will discuss. This will make it easier for everyone to follow along.

If you feel like you cannot use less than ten slides, then you might need to go back and refine your message. Every decision in the world can be described in less than 10 slides. Personally, I've used 10 slides or less to help CEOs make decisions involving billions. If those decisions can be put onto 10 slides, then you can do the same!

Chapter 7: The Fear Factor

We have all heard it; people would rather be dead than speak in public. 78% of people suffer from speech anxiety, which must mean 4/5 people on here would rather be in the casket than giving the eulogy. Why is that?

To understand that, we need to first reframe what fear really is.

When you think of public speaking what are the worst-case scenarios that spring to mind?

You freeze and forget everything (generally people's biggest fear); fear your talk won't hit the mark; that you'll be exposing yourself as inadequate; NOT being an expert…being judged!

Your fears have an underpinning premise, just like everything in life. Fear is, in most cases, the inability to handle a situation. The inability to handle it stems from either a lack of skill in a given situation or being in an area too advanced for your current situation.

Let me ask you this... If you had somehow found yourself in a situation where you had to give open heart surgery to someone right here right now, what would you do?

You would probably go through a raft of emotions fear, panic, anxiety etc. Why?

Because you lack the skill having never learnt or performed the procedure before.

If, however, you happen to be the world's leading cardio surgeon, you would likely pick up the required equipment and calmly get on with the job.

What about if you a recreational basketballer who suddenly finds themselves somehow running around in the NBA finals? Of course, it ridiculous, but imagine how you would feel. You are out of your league trying to compete with the best without having the skills, knowledge of plays, or a system to follow.

Here's the thing; this is exactly how it is when you step foot in front of a boardroom or onto a stage. You are setting yourself up for failure without the right tools in the kit. But it doesn't have to be that way. But before I give you the AHA moment on why it doesn't, we need to further drive home why we need to reframe our fears towards public speaking.

How many of you could ride a two-wheeled bike well the first time you jumped on it as a kid? No instruction, no transition from training wheels; you just jumped straight on and boom you had it as though you were a natural.

Of course, none of you could. We first needed to learn how to steer, then how to peddle with training wheels; then once we had those parts of the system down, we could then transition to learning how to balance and control it. Even after we did this, we still haven't ended up as Tour de France riders.

To get to that level we must further hone our skills and practice to get to the top echelon. The exact same happens with public speaking. None of us jump up and are naturally ready to confidently address a handful, hundreds, or even a whole cluster of people.

During a lot of our day to day lives, we see TV hosts, youtubers and celebrities delivering outstanding performances; but it is not often that we see poor speeches or presentations; and for good reason. This causes a complex in many of us who think if we can't do it 'perfect', we shouldn't get up and try to do it at all.

When it comes to effective public speaking, there is no 'the gift of the gab' or being 'fast on your feet'. Even if day to day you think some people have those attributes, it doesn't necessarily lead to a great presentation with an impactful message. Often, it generally leads to a lot of unnecessary words and a confused audience. The thing is though, for most of us, we don't get to go through the training wheel phase of speaking like we do riding a bike.

Unfortunately, most of us learn our skills in English class; often from teachers who aren't great speakers themselves. That teaching usually results in writing an essay on cue cards and reading it off word for word, which, in speaking terms is the equivalent of learning to ride a unicycle downhill. No one wants to watch it, as we all know it's going to end up messy.

So, what if we all reframed our fear of speaking and understand that it's actually a just a lack of a specific skill and a lack of a proven framework to follow? Understanding that just like when learning to ride a bike, if we were to learn this framework, we can all get to where we want to be as speakers. Best of all, with the right guidance, you can fast-track the journey and avoid those nasty crashes along the way.

When we provide a path to success we empower ourselves and take the power back that fear has had over us.

As we start to eliminate your fear and you simultaneously build up your confidence. Think about how difficult it is to be confident when you are fearful. Even if your exterior demeanour might show 'cool, calm and collected', your presentation will show the truth in some way. Initially, you will have more fear than confidence, but over time, being able to identify and mitigate that will flip that ratio around.

After our bungee jump, the confidence we all had was through the roof, mainly due to adrenaline more than mastering the task. Immediately after the jump we all went back to the front desk and negotiated a deal with the staff.

In exchange for a poorly choreographed dance to Nelly Furtado's Promiscuous Girl song, which was big at the time, they agreed to give us a discount on the Tshirts, photos and DVDs. It made them all laugh so much and entertained the tourists who just hopped off the bus, that they ended up giving it to us all for free.

You can check out the footage of the dance here: https://www.youtube.com/watch?v=ZTdMxsVruOM

Once you confront your fears you can then build on that experience to improve each time.

Initially, you will get a rush and a feeling of relief. Over time, the more talks you deliver (well), the more people you impact, and the greater success you will have that those feelings will turn into fulfilment, inner confidence, and gratitude.

As you develop as a speaker using a repeatable system, your consistency will improve. With that, confidence continues to grow, and you begin to push your new boundaries even further; allowing you to find your style and see what works with your audiences. Imagine how empowered you will feel after you nail each speech. The confidence boost will make you feel literally 10cm taller!

Very much how bungee instructors who have jumped hundreds of times become more fearless and produce more exciting jumps that challenge them even further each time.

Chapter 8: Foreplay

Now I was ready to try it out in front of the all-important decision-makers of TEDxBasel. According to our schedule, this was the final rehearsal at which we would be allowed to read from a script.

When I arrived at the meeting venue that was commandeered from another of Basel's companies, the room was already strewn with half-eaten pizzas. Three of my fellow speakers were there, two of whom had already rehearsed in front of Jane, Harrison, and a couple of the other volunteers, including my coach, Martin.

I'd arrived in time to hear the rehearsal of a stand-up comic based in Zurich. I was immediately mesmerised by him, given the size of his ample biceps. His amusing routine was promptly mauled by Harrison and Jane, who told him it belonged in a late-night comedy club and was wholly inappropriate for a TEDx audience. Rather than re-work his script then, they told him they would work on it with him another time so that they could fit in my rehearsal.

I belted out the latest version of my script, confident with how it had progressed.

"Far too loud... too much energy", came the feedback from Harrison.

I had clearly been too confident with my content. You will recall that the topic of my talk was about corporate jargon, commonly referred to in the business world as bullshit. My talk had included the use of this word, but only in the correct context. I've always taught my children only to use swear words when absolutely necessary; otherwise, they lose their impact and we'd have nothing left to use when we're next sewing on a button or fitting a new toilet seat.

"Next time, could you try it without using the word bullshit?", asked Jane.

"Can I ask why?", I enquired.

"Well, we are both teachers and we like to show the talks to our classes afterwards. If you use that word, we can't show it. Besides that, when your talk is published online, you will miss out on hits from American audiences", she answered.

"But my talk is about bullshit. It would seem odd not to name it. And I wrote it for an audience of adults, not schoolchildren."

"Just try saying B.S. instead. It'll be just the same", she insisted.

Harrison then proceeded to take us through the importance of memorising our speeches word-for-word. He did this by reading out the words on a PowerPoint presentation from one of the standard slide decks that TEDx organisers appear to be issued with.

I chose to continue trusting their process, even though I knew that memorising scripts hasn't been a strong point for me in the past. Otherwise, I might've considered going into acting.

At the final dress rehearsal for the organisers, back up in the industrial setting where we'd had our first speakers' meeting, I'd almost got the whole 11 minutes memorised. But almost isn't good enough when you're delivering a speech, and like all the other speakers who rehearsed that night, I found myself stumbling over familiar, memory-blocking phrases.

I wasn't yet at the "happy birthday" stage, as Harrison called it: the point where you can recite your speech while you're doing something else, like the washing up, just like everyone can sing "happy birthday" the whole way through while cooking eggs. Even men.

I'd replaced the bullshit word with alternatives wherever it made sense and left just one for the desired impact.

"You're in good shape", came the comment from Jane. "But I'd still like you to try it without that word, and see if it works. I don't think it will lose anything."

She hadn't made a murmur when the previous speaker's Italian accent had made the pronunciation of Immanuel

Kant's surname sound like something even more offensive.

In the week leading up to The Big Day, I was rehearsing with anyone who would listen: fellow trainers, training groups, other colleagues, friends via FaceTime, myself in the car, my children. My ten-year-old daughter helped me to remember the words by visualising parts of the speech with actions. Her way of demonstrating the phrase "helicopter view" was quite comical.

I rehearsed with an old friend, Matthew, via Skype. He gave me a scathing review, which hurt. This reaction surprised me because by this point I was sure I had a winning speech. In what must have been an "ignore-it-and-it'll-go-away" self-defence mechanism, I promptly blocked out his comments.

Lucy Kellaway, the former Financial Times columnist, said in an article referring to her TEDx talk, "all the faffing and rehearsing that TED demands had the effect of making me a cheesy, stilted version of myself." I was blind to the fact that this was happening to me.

The following day my good friend and fellow trainer, O'Patrick Wilson, made me listen to my own speech for me to really hear myself, and he pointed out my "poppy seed".

"This is not you", he told me. "Peter, I know you too well and what's coming out now is just not you. It's not natural. This whole thing has somehow undermined your confidence."

He was right. With all the pressure I'd put on myself and with the strict TED process, I'd become a "cheesy, stilted version of myself", just as Kellaway found.

Memorising the speech word for word was becoming a big stumbling block for me, particularly with a script that had other people's words infringing upon my own. It was at those points where I was encountering difficulty: the places where other people had put words in my mouth.

There was nothing else for it. I had to make the words my own. With only two days to go, I forfeited the speakers' dinner to go through my talk again with O'Patrick. O'Patrick is an excellent trainer who wasn't afraid to push me hard, as all good trainers should. We stripped out the stumbling blocks one by one and, thanks to his partner, Kirsty, added the finishing touch to the talk's punchline.

After almost six months of preparation, finally I felt ready.

The technical rehearsal at the venue itself – the Musical Theatre in Basel – was when it all became real. Having graced the stage on many occasions in the past as part of my work, I knew what to expect and the details I should look out for.

I stood in the centre of the famous TED red carpet and scoped out my stage space. Much to Jane's obvious irritation, I insisted on having a confidence monitor (where the speaker can see what's projected on the screen while facing the audience) installed at the foot of the stage so that I could read the projected examples I would show. These were far too complex for me to memorise. I also insisted on having a stool at the side of the stage from where I could pick up the slide advancer rather than having to hold this rather large device all the way through my speech.

The night before The Big Day, my 15-year-old son, Eric, who would be accompanying me to the event, endured six recitals: three times with "B.S." instead of "bullshit" and three times with "bullshit" uttered once, in the right place.

"There's only one thing for it Dad", said Eric. "You're going to have to say bullshit tomorrow."

And so I did.

Chapter 9: Great Ideas For Openings In Your Speech

A great speech always begins with a captivating opening. But how do you find a good one? To come up with a great opening, reflect on the main topic of your speech and try to find an introduction that can connect with it. You want your catchy introduction to grab attention and then naturally flow into the main content of your speech. Here are some ideas for what to use for great openings, and where to find them:

If you have a funny personal story that's related, share it to start off. People will naturally connect with you, especially if it's a funny or embarrassing story.Another strategy to find great stories, if you don't have one of your own is to share someone else's story. Research people who have done something great or unusual in connection with your topic and share their story as a way to get started. Stories engage your audience and they are more likely to remember the story that you told to make a point than an interesting detail you shared. Stories help people to connect emotionally with you.

If it's hard to find a story that fits, you can also research great quotes online to share. Search the internet for relevant quotes, or swing by the library and skim through some books with famous quotes. These words will inspire your audience and create a desire for them to learn more about what you have to say.

Are you a naturally funny person? How about sharing a great joke as your opener? Laughing is great way for people to bond together, and will increase the level of energy and excitement in your presentation. If you have a great joke that's appropriate, this is a great way to open your speech. Once everyone's done laughing, find a way to connect it to your topic and launch into your speech.

Lastly, another way to create a great opener is to use something from the current news or issues of today. If it's a particular season or holiday, you can use an interesting tidbit or fact that may surprise or intrigue your audience. Maybe there is a natural disaster that recently occurred and caused you to reflect on what you are grateful for. You can use this to connect into the message of your speech. Using current news or issues will engage your audience with what is going on in the real world today and show them that what you have to say is relevant to their lives.

Overall, when preparing an opening for your speech, don't feel pressured to always give your own personal story. There are tons of great stories, metaphors, quotations, jokes, real-life examples out there and feel free to use them! Your audience will begin to connect with you on an emotional level with a great opening and be drawn in to pay attention to the rest of your speech. Take time to create an excellent opening; it may be the most difficult part of your speech to write and discover, but will set the stage for the rest of the message you want to share.

Chapter 10: Consider The Purpose Of Your Presentation

In the introduction, I eluded to a 10-minute presentation. Obviously, there are a myriad of presentations that you may find yourself tackling throughout your life. Some of these presentations you will make by your own volition and others will be assigned to you. In my experience, making a presentation where you are not comfortable or knowledgeable about the subject matter will have a more negative, lasting impact. We will discuss this in more detail in a later chapter. Whether you step up to the plate and proactively make a presentation or somebody asks you to make a presentation, you have the opportunity to influence others.

In your 10-minute presentation, you will want to decide what your purpose is and create your presentation to convey that to your audience.

Here are some purposes you will want to use:

1. Informative: An example of this type of presentation is if you were to present a new product, service, procedure and/or policy in the work environment. This presentation will typically write itself. You did not make the product or service. You did not create the procedure or policy. This is yet another opportunity to show off your skills in delivering information. These types of presentations help you to be seen by people in your organization who are looking for talent to promote. They are looking for individuals who can clearly and concisely communicate with confidence. These presentations should be added as accomplishments to your annual performance review and will look great on your resume.

2. Instructional: In this type of presentation, you will give directions or orders. This would be more of a workshop or seminar, as you will need time to cover the topic thoroughly. In an instructional presentation, your objective is to have the audience/participants come away with a new skill or knowledge. I am confident that you've attended this type of presentation.

Your first step in an instructional presentation is to explain why the information or skill is valuable to the audience. Capturing their attention at the beginning of your presentation by giving them a benefit for listening will set the right tone for the entire presentation. Next, give them a very brief outline on how the presentation will flow. There will be more tips in the chapter titled "Content" that will help you set up the flow of any presentation. Participants in a workshop/seminar setting want to be involved and you want to make sure they've mastered (or are at least comfortable) with the new skill(s) you've introduced to them.

Once you've taught the new skill, have them practice the skill. You definitely want to reserve time for participants to ask questions along the way, and give and receive feedback from you and other participants. Also, make sure the participants can realistically use the new skill in their life by sharing how they will do this.

3. Persuasive: Your purpose here is to persuade your audience that your topic is so important that they should jump on board. You would do this with logic, emotion, and evidence to back up your point. I have a friend who believes that every man, woman, and child should include five servings of fruits and vegetables in their day. I've seen him make presentations in my local community in several different venues. When you leave the presentation, he has a handout of some of his favorite recipes where you can substitute vegetables for meat that you would normally use. Let me tell you how persuasive he is. For about four weeks after I see him make this presentation, I eat more fruits and vegetables than I did in the previous six months. I also become much more physically active when I attend a presentation where the speaker is persuading me to get off that couch and start moving!

4. Stimulating: The objective of this type of presentation is to give a call to action. A great example would be a speech at a fundraiser. You want people to open that checkbook and contribute! These tend to have emotion included to tug at the hearts of participants. Don't just tell me why I should participate in your request; tell me what happens if I don't.

5. Entertain: Perhaps you've been asked to honor somebody at a retirement function because you know that person well and can, with respect, say a few words that will simply entertain the audience. Or perhaps you've been asked to toast the bride and groom at their reception because your friends know the audience will be entertained by your contribution. Perhaps you've been asked to talk about your team's success at work to other employees. You could give the information and entertain the audience at the same time. However, most work-related presentations will fall under the Inform and/or Instruct type. There are many opportunities to entertain audiences while speaking. This is not a typical type of presentation you will make. I could be wrong. Perhaps you'd like to be a stand-up comedian.

6. Inspire/Motivate: These presentations are meant to move your audience. They are meant to inspire them to achieve their goals in life. Joel Osteen is a very inspiring and motivating speaker. The passion he brings to his presentations moves people to appreciate everything they have in their lives. I'm sure there are many people that you are thinking of right now who inspire and motivate others with their words.

Martin Luther King, Jr, Susan B. Anthony, and Abraham Lincoln shared their passion in a way that moved people to aspire to greatness. Most of the time, people are inspired when they hear about a person who's overcome hardship and adversity. Helen Keller comes to mind in this category.

Eulogies can be very inspiring. You may be asked to or volunteer to pay tribute to someone that you know and love who has passed away. Probably more than any other type of presentation, this is one you will want to write down. Every word. Practice it beforehand to ensure you can say the words and manage the emotion. The most moving eulogy I have ever heard was presented by a 13-year old girl whose father had taken his own life. She loved her father very much. She did not understand why he would choose to take his own life and did not focus on that during her tribute. Her parents were going through a bitter divorce and she and her twin sister were pinned right in the middle of the crises. This young lady wrote the most beautiful tribute to her "hero." Every person in the audience was in tears as this young lady spoke with her head held high in a strong and clear voice. It was truly inspiring.

Chapter 11: Body Language Techniques For Public Speaking

If you want to find the truth, do not listen to the words coming to you. Rather see the body language of the speaker. It speaks the facts not audible. - Bhavesh Chhatbar

Body language is an essential part of public speaking success. Your non-verbal cues will impact on the way your message is received, how engaged your audience is, and what they think of you as an individual. Even if you've prepared the best speech in the world, if you aren't animated, open or active then your audience won't know what you've said.

Below are some Body Language Techniques that can help you make a big difference in your Public Speaking drive.

Eye contact

Making eye contact with your audience builds a connection between you and them and they feel more valued by you. Establishing eye contacts with your audience can reveal their emotions to you as a speaker and this can help you adjust your presentations.

Hand and arm Gesture Hand gestures are one of the best ways we use to communicate our words to an audience confidently when used correctly, hand and arm gestures can help enhance your message and make you seem more confident and relaxed. You can use hand gestures to emphasize your words and regain your strength during presentations.

Movement on stage

Moving around the stage is a great way of showing your audience you are confident in what you're saying, moving on stage will help you relax your body and also connect with your audience directly

Use a loud, projecting voice

Your vocal expression is physical and so your body language has an effect on your voice and can enhance or detract from the message of your speech.

Pay attention to your Mannerisms

Mannerisms are the nervous habits most people have that detract from your message and can make the audience feel uncomfortable

Facial expression

The movements of your eyes, mouth, and facial muscles can build a connection with your audience. Alternatively, they can undermine your every word. Eye focus is the most important element in this process. No part of your facial expression is more important in communicating sincerity and credibility.

Stay out of the way of the projector lights.

Whenever you are delivering your presentation make sure to avoid crossing the Projector lights. You need to position yourself in search a way that you don't block the view of your audience

Chapter 12: Contexts Of Public Speaking

Any public address is hollow, meaningless, and incomplete if there is no clear context. If the context is not defined, then it will be impossible for the audience to get what you are saying. The entire process of speaking in front of an audience will become an effort in vain without context. Also, if the context is not well-established or well-defined, it will be difficult for you, as the speaker to understand your audience, their needs, and their reactions.

Contexts: Situational and Environmental

While audience is truly an important consideration in making your speech and molding your message, you should also put as one of your primary considerations the given context. In determining the context, one of the factors is the type of audience and the characteristics of its members. But audience is just one of the many factors that have to be considered.

Have you ever experienced accidentally listening to an ongoing conversation while you are walking through a hallway? While you might have caught three to five sentences, it is likely that whatever you have heard, you will not be able to make sense or derive meaning from it. The issue here, therefore, is not completeness of thought. What you have missed in this particular instance is the context by which the conversation was made. Moving on to the delivery of public speeches, it is therefore important to make sure that you and your audience are on the same page and both are under the same context so that the exchange of information will be meaningful.

Situational context pertains to the real motive behind you speaking or presenting in front of an audience. For example, if you are a senatorial candidate, your situational context is that you want to convince people who are registered voters to vote for you in the upcoming election. On the other hand, if you are the best man at a wedding, you might be asked to deliver a speech under the situational context that you want to express your best wishes to the newly-weds. Lastly, if you are at a funeral, your speech should be a eulogy based on the underlying situational context which is to express grief and loss.

Therefore, the manner of delivery and the content of the speech heavily relies on the situational context. This will prevent you from saying a best man's speech at a funeral. Also, it will give you a hint regarding the appropriate tone or manner by which you will deliver your speech.

Environmental context, on the other hand, represents the venue in which you will deliver your speech. This greatly influences both your manner of delivery and even your actual message. The environmental context for a public speech may vary in terms of size and structure.

Your success as a speaker may be enhanced or stalled by environmental context and how you adjust to it. But a skilled public speaker is able to maximize whatever environmental context is given to him. A good speaker has a keen sense of situational awareness because he keeps his eyes, ears, heart, and mind open at all times. Once you are aware about your environment, most likely, you will know how to proceed.

Responding to environmental context can be very challenging because it requires a person to be aware of the situation at all times. This can only be done if you are observant minute by minute. By doing this, you can predict all possible changes in the environment that you may encounter during the delivery of the speech. By being on top of the situation at all times, you can be a step ahead and you will successfully adapt to the situation. It is quite challenging to hone this particular skill, so you will need a lot of practice.

Understanding Culture and Gender

First and foremost, it is important for you to understand that culture and race are two different things. Race pertains to the groups that are sharing a set of commonalities: physical traits, type of hair, and the color of the skin. Therefore, race is manifested by the on-the-surface traits. On the other hand, culture pertains to something deeper – habits, traditions, morals, values, and customs. Take note that though they are closely related, culture and race are two different things.

Meanwhile, gender is not only about the genitalia that a person possesses. It goes beyond that. Gender is actually a sociological construct that is distinguished by a set of values, behaviors, and ideals. While sex is to male and female, gender is to masculine and feminine.

Bias is a commonly encountered issue when you meddle with culture and gender contexts. Bias can either be explicit or implicit, intentional or unintentional. Our judgments differ on the individual level, so if you are a speaker, you should be very careful with the way you deliver points that are related to this. As much as possible, you should avoid offending any group of people.

When you tackle topics of any issue, it is ideal that you remove your biases. Though this is not possible, at least you should try to minimize your bias.

To avoid issues that might compromise your intention as a public speaker, the best thing to do is to know your audience first. What you will do next will depend on that heavily.

Chapter 13: We All Have To Go On The Stage

So many times people say this,"I don't want to learn public speaking or why I should learn public speaking? I don't like going on the stage. I'm very happy in my life. I'm doing good in my work."

Someone has to define the word STAGE. STAGE doesn't mean that big stage where you're standing and then you are speaking in front of thousands of people.

STAGE is something else. I remember I was speaking in one school. Sharing some stories with children and that school was in the interior of Maharashtra and very small. So small that in that school there was no stage.

While sharing stories I asked one question "Tell me when was the last time you were standing on the stage?" And one girl raised hand, her name was Aarti and she said "Sir, there is no stage in the school" I asked one question and the answer to that question might help you to understand what does stage really mean.

I said "Aarti, just imagine for a moment that after the school when you reach home, you open the door and you see along with your parents there are seven to eight guests sitting at your home. Now you were not expecting those guests. Your mom when she looks at you she gets excited and she says "yeah my daughter Aarti has come and you know she is very good at reciting poems. Aarti will you please stand there and recite one poem for us", Suddenly you realize you're

standing in front of seven to eight people and somehow you are not feeling comfortable. The only reason you are feeling uncomfortable at that particular moment because you're standing on the STAGE".

Whenever you separate yourself from the crowd, doesn't matter where that crowd is maybe that crowd is in your office, in your small group meeting, maybe that crowd in your big annual meeting or maybe that crowd is at your family gathering, and whenever you separate yourself from the crowd irrespective of the audience size, irrespective of where exactly the audience is sitting, that is the STAGE.

And speaking on the stage is a learnable skill, just like singing and dancing, we have to learn and practice speaking from the stage.

Why you should learn how to speak on the stage? Only for one reason if you want to become a leader in your life. Because if you want to be a leader you have to separate yourself from the crowd, stand alone and speak.

6. Are you just 7% ready with your

presentation or speech

Most of us make presentations. Imagine for a moment that you have a presentation tomorrow. what will you do? Most of the time you will spend the whole day and sometimes the whole night in making that PPT. You will find some best content to make that PPT and the next morning when you

are standing in front of people you are only seven percent ready. Why seven percent?

Albert Mehrabian, he did a big study on communication many experts say that the outcome of this study is the fundamental of communication whenever we are standing in front of people.

It says that there are three components which decide the effectiveness of communication, whenever we are speaking from the stage. Number 1- of course, the content, number

2- body language, number 3-vocal variety. But in this study, he has given the percentage of each component as per their contribution toward effective communication.

Many times I ask people to guess the percentages and most of the time they give the maximum percentage to the content.

As per this study, the content is only 7 %, body language is 55

% and vocal is 38 %. So it means 93 % of what decides the effectiveness of communication, we don't practice.

But does that mean, the content is not important? Of course NOT. Content is important, content is the king. But what it means that even if you have the world's best content or world's best PPT or world's best story but if your body language and vocal variety are not good you might not be able to communicate effectively.

Chapter 14: I See Over 80% Of Speakers Make These Two Mistakes

One indicator that tells me that a person is an effective speaker within the first two seconds of the speech is an extremely easy one to spot. That indicator is the volume of the speaker's voice. I usually know right away if someone is probably not a good speaker. If the volume of their voice is slightly too quiet, or even at the level of a normal conversational volume, that is a dead giveaway to me that the speech is probably going to be a boring one. On the other hand, if the speaker's voice is too loud, that is a dead giveaway to me that the speaker thinks he or she is a great speaker, but in reality, really isn't. A loud speaker sounds arrogant, possibly stupid, and sometimes will bore you as well. There are exceptions to the rule, such as the comedian Sam Kinison, who was famous for incorporating loud shouting and yelling into his acts. Remember that he was only able to do this because standup comedy follows similar, but very different rules at the same time when it comes to public speaking. Also, he was a paid professional, so he knew what he was doing. Even then, he only yelled and shouted at a loud volume at **parts** of his performance, and did not do so for every word and sentence that he spoke. When I discuss the volume of the voice in this lesson, I'm really talking about the overall volume that you are using for most of the words and sentences that you say.

So what is the best volume that will most likely get an audience's attention right from the beginning? The best level of volume for your voice should be one that is a tinge higher than a medium level. Take whatever you consider to be a normal sounding voice, and add just a little bit to it. The key is to not overdo it, but not give enough either. Let's say that if you were to measure the loudest shout that you could possibly muster on a scale of 0 to 100, the shout would be a 100, the quietest whisper you could produce at 0, and a normal conversational volume at 50, then I want you to speak at a volume of 54-58. A number of 63-65 is far too high, but is good if you really wish to emphasize an important point in your speech, and a number of 40-50 is too low unless you want to de-emphasize a certain point in your speech.

The volume of your voice might be a troublesome thing to control if you don't like the sound of your voice. Some of the best speakers in the past didn't have pleasant sounding voices, such as Abraham Lincoln. Don't worry about it if you don't think you have a pleasant sounding voice because it's not necessary for doing a good speech. Focus on rehearsing the volume and control of your voice as you practice.

When done properly in front of an audience, a strong, but not too powerful voice will let the people know in their subconscious minds, that they are listening to someone who probably knows what they are talking about, and therefore is not going to waste their time. Assuming your audience consists almost entirely of people whom you do not personally know, this is an excellent way to instantly illuminate yourself on the stage. If you do happen to know the people in the audience, and it is a small audience, I would recommend a level of volume that falls between 50 and 53.

Another mistake that I see many speakers make is that they fail to properly initiate eye contact with the audience as soon as they get behind the podium, or in front of the audience. Big mistake. I'm not going to explain why eye contact makes an audience more interested or more disinterested depending on how you use it because I don't know. What I do know is that it's just something that works. There could be pages written about how to utilize eye contact to your advantage, just like how pages can be written on how the volume of your voice is a critical aspect to public speaking, and how body language, usage humor, and a plethora of other things are critical too. That's because each of these individual aspects of public speaking are a sort of art within themselves.

Eye contact is just as much of an art as public speaking also being a sort of art. Imagine that -an art within an art. Who would've thought?

To begin, I'm going to suggest that as soon as you get on the stage, you need to aim your eyes somewhere in the general direction of the audience, but do not try to make eye contact with a particular individual unless you are answering a question from him or her. Failure to make eye contact with an audience as soon as you begin to say your first word indicates to them that you're not exactly quite sure if you have anything useless or entertaining to say. It also indicates that you may possibly not even be concerned about whether you perform well or not, or that you may not even care about what you have to say. If you don't look like you care about what you have to say, then the audience isn't going to care either.

Imagine when you were young and there was something really exciting that you wanted to discuss with your parents or your friends. It could've been about a new toy that you wanted, or something of that nature. Try and recapture that energy that existed within you at that moment in your life (minus the excessive smiling and bouncing around), and translate it into making firm eye contact with the audience.

Another thing about eye contact is that it is always a good idea to sustain it for as long as possible. To make this action not look awkward, simply scan the audience with your eyes left to right while you speak. Now, you might be wondering, what if I need to look down at my notes or pieces of paper while I speak? This is where things get a little tricky, but nobody said that public speaking is easy, right? The solution is to still try to keep your head up as much as possible while you are speaking, and trying not to spend more than three or four seconds at a time when you need to see what you're going to talk about next.

Before I get into more elaborate details on how to take advantage of the power of eye contact, keep in mind that the ideas that I have just provided in the last few paragraphs are sufficient enough to help make a great speech. You could stop right here with your learning of eye contact techniques and still do very well. But, if you wish to learn more, then proceed to the next paragraph where I will mention just a couple of more things. I just don't want to give you too much information to digest at once, and put more pressure on you to change this and that so that in the end, you make no real progress in your public speaking abilities. One thing I should mention about this book is that it's a good idea to take things slowly, and learn no more than two things a day at a time.

Okay, so here's a neat trick you can do with an audience to make yourself appear more interesting. I don't know why exactly it works, I just know that it does.

The next time you are giving a speech, try staring towards the back of the room, and keep your head up slightly high, as if you were looking for someone in the back. When you do this, keep looking at the back of the room for a while, preferably at least ten seconds. You could even do it for minutes. This technique is a very subtle one that accomplishes a very subtle effect. By looking at the back of the room, it gives the front and middle part of the audience the illusion that you are directing your speech towards someone else that is not them, and as a result, those in the front and middle will feel like they are eavesdropping on some sort of conversation or dialogue. Hey, who doesn't like to eavesdrop? The irony is that the whole time, everyone in the audience can clearly hear what you are saying. It's amazing how subtle tactics such as this actually work.

Finally, I'm going to talk about a time when it's actually appropriate that you look downwards instead up towards an audience. It's a bit difficult to explain when to do this, but it's a lot easier once you see someone else do it. Basically, it's a good idea to look downwards when you are elaborating something in your speech that you had forgotten to mention earlier. However, when you do this, only look downwards for a split second. Any longer, and it will look awkward. The purpose of this effect is that it makes you look like a humble person, and anytime you manage to make convince the audience that you are humble, you will make your image skyrocket. What I mean is that being humble gives the audience another reason to love what you are saying, and as a result, more interested in what you have to say. If you are unsure as to how to pull this off in your next speech, then by all means don't try it. Just remember it.

Chapter 15: Dealing With Glossophobia Or The Fear Of Public Speaking

In case you feel that your fear of public speaking is more serious that it seems then you will have to find a different course of management and treatment. The good news is that these types of presentation anxieties can be easily managed with the help of different treatment methods. These treatment methods won't eat up a lot of time since they are only short term treatments. A couple of popular treatment methods include Systematic Desensitization and the other one is called cognitive Behavioral Therapy.

Take note that you should take these courses of action in case your fear of public speaking has come to a point where the distress you feel is really significant. This means that it is already interfering with your normal course of life. If that is the case then you may talk to your family doctor and ask for a referral to a psychiatrist who can help you.

Understanding the Symptoms of Social Anxiety Disorder

Although only a trained professional can really identify whether a person has a SAD or not, it can help to know the symptoms. At least if you are aware of the said symptoms you can tell whether you need professional help or not.

Take note that people with SAD will react negatively when presented with situational triggers. They usually resent being humiliated or even embarrassed in front of other people. Giving is a speech is only one of the many social triggers that can induce anxiety in people with Social Anxiety Disorder. The other social triggers include job interviews, going on a date, telephone calls, eating in front of others, having a conversation, going to a party, athletic competitions, business conferences, musical performances, and work meetings.

Take note that all these social triggers have something to do with how the individual interacts with a crowd. They are typically scared of being seen in a negative light. But who wouldn't right? Well, for people with SAD their fears are carried way to far if compared to how we handle our own fears.

Experts have categorized the symptoms into three overarching classifications: physical symptoms, cognitive symptoms, and behavioral symptoms.

The Physical Symptoms of Social Anxiety Disorder

Most of us can also feel the same physical symptoms. However, when people with SAD experience these same symptoms they get extremely distressed. Their reaction is just beyond the way we usually react. Some of the common physical symptoms include disorientation, shaking, sweating, blushing, shortness of breath, a racing heart, muscle tension, dry mouth, and a trembling voice.

Cognitive Symptoms of SAD

When we talk about cognitive symptoms we are basically referring to how people think. Experts will look for dysfunctional thought patterns. These include thoughts of self-doubt and other negative thoughts with regard to the social stimuli or social triggers.

These negative thought patterns should be treated as soon as possible. Never let them go on since they never get better by themselves. They will continue to breed with the individuals until their self-esteem starts to erode.

They usually have a lot of negative bias about themselves. Instead of highlighting their own social capabilities they tend to dwell on and highlight the social capabilities of other people. Even the most positive social encounter that they experience will be taken in a darker more negative light.

Other than possessing that negative bias, people with SAD often are filled with negative thoughts. Their negative self-evaluations may sometimes seem so automatic that can't tell where it's coming from. Slightly related to negative thoughts are the person's negative beliefs. These are more than just thoughts or assertions about themselves. These are long held and strong beliefs about one's inadequacy with regard to the social encounter or situation in question.

Behavioral Symptoms of SAD

When we talk about behavioral symptoms these are more than just physical responses and they are more than just thoughts or beliefs. We are dealing with how people will actually react and behave when presented with social stimuli. Experts agree that people with SAD have a generally poor quality of life. This means that they have a few friends (or maybe none at all). They may have dropped out of school. They may have even opted out of romantic relationships. At the very extreme end of the spectrum some people with SAD may have turned to alcoholism just to cope with their anxieties.

They almost always behave in at least three different ways. The first reaction or behavior they have to social triggers is to avoid it altogether. It would be better for them to avoid being around the crowd. The second reaction is that they take the initiative and find ways to limit their social interactions with other people.

They rarely attend company parties, social gatherings, and close off ties with other folks. The last reaction or behavior is to simply flee from the social trigger that causes them a lot of anxiety. You ask them to give a five minute message in front of the congregation and they don't show up the following Sunday. You ask them to give the toast at the party and they disappear or don't show up at the party.

The Good News

There is good news for people who have SAD. Studies have shown that they respond very well to various forms of treatment. There are medications that can be used in the treatment process. Other than medication, there are also psychotherapy treatments available to people suffering from these symptoms. It's a very treatable condition and no one ought to suffer from them when such treatment is generally available.

Medications Available

There are available medications that therapists can use to treat SAD. The most common medications that are prescribed to such patients are selective serotonin reuptake inhibitors or SSRIs. Yes, some of these medications are also the same ones used to treat depression. These medications regulate a person's moods and eventually an individual's anxieties.

The following are the SSRIs that are recommended for treating SAD patients: Celexa (Citalopram), Zoloft (Sertraline), Lexapro (Escitalopram), Prozac (Fluoxetine), Luvox (Fluvoxamine), and Paxil (Paroxetine).

Take note that these medications are available by prescription. Remember to follow your doctor's instructions when taking any of these medications.

People who take these medications have reported the following side effects:

erectile dysfunction, weight gain, irritability, skin rashes, drowsiness, decreased sex drive, dry mouth, fatigue or insomnia, dizziness, sweating, delayed or absent orgasm, headaches, and nausea.

Take note that you shouldn't discontinue the use of SSRIs abruptly without the supervision of your doctor. Stopping their use abruptly may result in withdrawal symptoms and/or a relapse of anxiety symptoms.

What is Systematic Desensitization?

One of the psychiatric treatments used by therapists to treat public speaking anxiety and Glossophobia is called Systematic Desensitization. In this treatment method, the patient is asked to imagine the events that usually trigger the feelings of anxiety.

During the treatment the patient will also undergo a series of different relaxation exercises to help counter the anxiety symptoms. After some time the patient will become desensitized to the social trigger that causes the patient a deal of anxiety. Patients come out of treatment will less anxiety due to the said social trigger.

What is Cognitive Behavioral Therapy?

Cognitive Behavioral Therapy is not a single routine treatment that is used by therapists to treat speech anxiety or any other form of anxiety disorders. It is actually a combination of various treatments and techniques. Studies have shown that CBT is one of the most reliable forms of therapy when dealing with different types of anxiety disorders.

The combination of treatment techniques will ultimately depend on the type of phobia that the patient is experiencing. So there will be a different CBT approach to treating speech anxiety and a totally different approach when treating another form of anxiety.

There are several factors that will help determine the success of Cognitive Behavioral Therapy. One of these factors is the patient's willingness to complete assigned tasks. Without the participation of the individual the treatment will not be as successful. Another important factor that comes into play is the patients' capability to confront the very thoughts that causes them discomfort. The people who participate and are willing to work with the therapist in the treatment process will likely succeed and overcome their anxieties faster and so much better. Studies have shown that the results of these treatments tend to be long lasting if CBT becomes truly successful.

What is Exposure Therapy?

Exposure therapy is actually one of the many techniques employed in Cognitive Behavioral Therapy (CBT). It is generally used to reduce the patient's fear with regard to certain situational stimuli (such as giving a speech for instance). The main idea with this treatment approach is to expose the individual to the situation insomuch that the patient becomes so used to the experience that it doesn't trigger the same degree of anxiety as before.

Exposure therapy often uses a couple of different types of exposures. Sometimes the exposure to the said situational trigger will be intense and fast. The patient is typically exposed to the said social trigger quite rapidly. That is a totally different approach compared to Systematic Desensitization, which basically incorporates gradual exposure which is thereafter followed by relaxation exercises.

Work with Your Therapist

The important thing in any treatment method is your willingness to work with someone who is more than willing to help you. Once you recognize the symptoms of a more serious condition other than a simple nervousness over a speaking engagement it is in your best interest to seek help immediately. The longer these conditions remain untreated the greater the eventual damage to one's life and well-being will be. This is a serious matter and if you see someone exhibiting the said symptoms then it will be in the interest of that friend that you will come to his or her aid.

Chapter 16: Use Your "Crutches"

The final thing that you need to become a master speaker is what I call the "crutch". Your crutches are actually the visual aids that you use when you present your speech. Crutches involve all sorts of tools including PowerPoint presentations, group interactions, key materials, audience volunteers, short videos and even recorded information. There are a lot of these aids that you can utilize in order to spice up your presentation and most importantly be there if you need them during your talk.

In the medical field, the most common aid that instructors utilize are the demonstrations. Most students tend to see live presentations of medical techniques during lectures. Through seeing the actual techniques, the students will be able to pick out the right procedures so that they will be able to practice it during their time inside the hospital. This is also true when it comes to other occupations and studies.

Of course, modern technology has also made a huge advancement in public speaking. Nowadays, speakers present their topics through the use of visual presentations aimed with the key information including the use of graphs and pictures. Since PowerPoint presentations can be edited with sound and animations, your listeners will remain engaged once they see your templates. Remember to only include the necessary data in your presentations and use a laser pointers in order to present important facts.

Sometimes, speakers tend to ask questions to the crowd in order to get more information. Group interactions improve the relationship between the speaker and the crowd. It is also a great way for speakers to grab some information and ideas from his listeners. If you plan to use this strategy then remember to make it as short and as simple as possible and never ask questions that are too complicated. You should also never ask questions which are too personal.

If your listeners are children or when you are presenting something based on music, then you need interactive media. Short videos and audio tracks will help you entertain your young audience while at the same time it will provide you with more time to compose your next topic. Make sure that you use videos which are applicable for your age group.

Finally, if your presentation is based on a certain procedure or a group based topic then you can utilize audience volunteers. Audience volunteers are effective especially when you want to present a certain technique with the crowd. Magicians actually utilize audiences in order to make their presentations more believable. Just like a magician, you can ask an audience member to help present a fact or to practice a certain procedure. Make sure that if you are using an audience member your instructions should be clear and straight to the point.

There are other aids that you can utilize for your presentation, and they all depend on your topic. If you will be using other visual aids then make sure that they can wow your audience and that they are relevant to your presentation. Make sure that those "crutches" you use are fully prepped before your big act.

Chapter 17: Writing Your Material

"To me, genius is 1% inspiration and 99% good writers."

George Burns

• Know Your Audience

So, you've been hired to give a talk to some group or other. Now you're ready to write your speech. Before you do, don't think about the speech, think about the audience. What do you know about them? You see, every speech, talk or presentation is a call to action of some sort. What's the call to action for your little gem? When you've finished, what do you want the audience to do? Another way of saying it, "What will they miss if they don't act?"

We dealt with this a bit back in the Message section. Now, the focus is on the audience. Ask these questions before you get into writing the material:

1. Who are they? What do you know about the group that invited you to speak? What do you need to know about them? What is their background? Age range? Income range? Are they business people? Technical people? Financial types? Secretaries? Jockeys? Doctors? Lawyers? Indian Chiefs? Are they students? Retirees? Where do they live? Work? Do they have kids? Grandkids? Pets? Slaves? (There's a more complete checklist in a few pages.)

2. Concerns? What are their chief issues or trepidations regarding your topic/product/service? How much do they know about it?

3. Competitors? If you have a business focus, what (if anything) do you need to know about their rivals?

4. Honchos? Who are the decision-makers or leaders in this group? How can you better gear your talk to meet satisfy their agenda?

This information isn't hard to come by. You can usually get it from the group's program chairperson or other officers, a talkative secretary, the library, industry or company publications, maybe the Internet, etc.

• Become the Audience

If you really want to get a clear idea of what the audience might want from being with you and hearing your dynamic presentation, pretend you're part of the audience. Be truthful with yourself, as an audience member, what do you really want? To learn something valuable, to network, to schmooze, to get a competitive edge, to show off, to catch on fire about work, to take time off work, to be entertained, to improve image, to score points with the boss, to get out of the rain, to have a great meal, to not be bored, to rest your weary bones, to buy something, to join something, to get more business, to attract more clients, to sharpen a skill, to be convinced about your idea, project or plan, to kill time, to get to know that sexy file clerk better.

• Speech Checklist

For any speech you're giving, know as much as you can about the following:

The Audience

1. Number of people you'll be speaking to? (Two, two hundred, too many?)

2. What are their occupations? (Car dealers, car salesmen, car thieves?)

3. Audience mix? (All men? All women? Mixed? Other???)

4. Age? (Teens, young adults, middle-age, geezers?)

5. Economic status? (White collar? Blue collar? Dog collar?)

6. General educational level? (High school grads, college grads, drop outs, drop ins?)

7. Cultural status? (Are they a classy group, or do they think that pro wrestling is culture?)

8. What fears and challenges are they currently facing? (Mergers? Downsizing? Y3K?)

9. What gives them _{joy?} (Company just won the industry softball tournament? Or, they just got bonuses? Or the big boss just broke his foot?)

10. What do they already know? (Of course about your subject, but also in general?)

11. What mindset will they be in (Upbeat? Down? Angry? Apathetic? Fish frenzy?)

12. What might be their _{attitude toward your speech} subject? (Does your speech challenge their status quo? Or reinforce what they think to be true? Or should you be prepared for a quick exit?) These are the balloons I was talking about.

13. What might be their attitude toward you as the speaker? (Receptive? Antagonistic? Blah?)

The Occasion

1. Purpose of the meeting? (This speech is a reward for a record-breaking quarter. Or, they just had the worst quarter ever, and management wants motivation — or maybe, revenge?)

2. Where will the meeting be held? (Conference room, auditorium, in a broom closet?)

3. Available facilities? (Lectern, overheads, microphone, AK-47?)

4. When will you give your talk? (Early morning? Afternoon? Evening? Middle of the night?)

5. What else is on the program? (If you're on right after the stripper, be prepared for lack of attention.)

6. What happens after your speech? (If you're on right before the stripper, be prepared to shorten your speech.)

7. What is the hoped-for outcome? (Management or speaker-sponsor goals for this speech: heightened communication among employees, more

effective leadership, agreement to slave wages?)

The Speaker

1. Do you have sufficient knowledge about your subject? (If not, how do you get it?)

2. Are you really interested in the your subject? (And you'd better be!)

3. Do you have enough preparation time ? (Sometimes, the only thing worse than not having enough preparation time is having too much.)

4. Will the audience accept you as a knowledgeable speaker? (If not — short of giving everybody a Rolex — what do you need to do to get this acceptance?)

Business Talk

If you're hired by a company to give speech, get to the top. Ask the highest executives that you have access to:

- What their biggest challenges are?
- What the company vision is?

- What they want improved from your program?

If you can also talk to members of the work force, ask them:

- What they like most about their jobs?
- What they're proudest of?
- What the problem areas are?
- The Challenges of Writing

"If anything can keep you from writing...let it!"

Bryce Courtney, author

If you know your topic, you know your audience, you know how you can benefit this particular audience...now, you're ready to write your speech/talk/presentation.

A few words about the ins and outs of writing. Especially if writing is not already a habit, regardless of the length of your speech or presentation, writing can be a very tricky process. It doesn't matter what you're writing, be it a book, a script, a speech or a report. Writing can be a pain. (Even checks aren't easy to write!) Every 100 words on paper equal about one spoken minute. This means that an hour-long speech is about 20 pages using the typeface you're reading now. 20 pages is more than the average person writes in one stretch in a lifetime. And you want it to be perfect, and you want it to sing, and you want it to be appropriate for the audience. No wonder, writing is the Godzilla of the creative arts!

Here are a few hints from a veteran writer and writing coach.

√ Vision

Make sure you know why you're starting this journey. Ask yourself what you want, and how soon you want it. Do you REALLY want it? Why do you want it? How is this speech or presentation going to change your life? How willing are you to make the changes necessary to make this dream happen? Why is it so damned important? You'll hang onto this answer when the going gets tough.

√ Commitment

The key is commitment. Most of us can get in touch with what we want that would make our lives better, more exciting, more prosperous. The tRICKY PART is digging into the primal goo to CREATE THE COMMITMENT NECESSARY to break through the habits, patterns and fear-based beliefs that stand in our way. How committed are you to making this monumental shift in your life?

Remember: 1) at least at the beginning, the writing COMMITMENT IS TO A CERTAIN NUMBER OF HOURS PER WEEK that you'll be sitting at your desk, writing utensils in hand, NOT TO any kind of OUTPUT. 2) anything that comes between you and that commitment is distraction. ANything!

√ Priorities

We all live 24 hours a day. If you start writing 10 hours a week, that 10 hours must come from somewhere. Something that you were doing before (time with children, clients, exercise, sleep) must drop off. In my experience working with people, it's not hard for most to declare their visions, not even hard to create a commitment. But when it comes to shifting priorities and facing the fear, doubt, diversion that naturally comes up in the process...ah, another story.

Anytime we go to the edges of our comfort zones to claim our dreams, the rock and roll is supposed to happen. If it doesn't, the chances are we're not really stepping out of our comfort zones.

√ Importance

The key question (that you may return over and over to as the going gets tough): is it important enough to change your life for? Is it important enough to change your relationships for? Is it important enough to change these relationships so that they support you in your writing process? Meaning: mates, friends and children happily work around your new schedules, your new priorities, the new phantom lover in your life?

There are usually three levels to the answer for these questions:

1) Career Impetus: What will having a well-crafted talk do for your PROFESSIONAL LIFE? How much more MONEY will it help you make? How will it enhance your FAME and RECOGNITION? How much more CREDIBILITY will you have? What will it LEAD TO?

2) New talent: All expression is a gift, but writing — reducing the universe to a letter at a time — is a most special one. Once one has unearthed their ability to express with words on paper, nothing is ever the same.

3) Personal breakthrough: There's nothing like writing (and completing) a book, play, script or speech to force one to meet the dragons, to step right up and give them a sloppy kiss. The territory between us and our dragons, demons and dratted devils is

mined with old, unexpressed pain, doubt and fear. Especially if the writing content is about one's life, the writing process is tailored to promote personal consciousness: mastery.

√ The Ritual

Because writing is translating the universe a letter at a time, sometimes there's a fair amount of grunt and groan. Nothing wants to work, the body isn't amenable, the spirit doesn't seem willing.

Your universe wants to support you in your creative effort. To help it along, develop a regular pattern. Write in the same time period, if possible. In the same place. Put gemstones, totems and other ritual items around. Bless the space. Put out a couple of glasses of water. Sit quietly before you begin, breathe, relax, enlist the devas and supportive muses to help the process along. Use instrumental music (headphones or not) to set the mood.

√ Style

You already have writing style. Good writing is not so much technique. Good writing is not so much dependent on education and background. Good writing is about communication. You already know how to communicate. The task is to give permission to your expression so that your inherent communication skills have a chance to flourish. You already have style. You've been developing it all your life. This natural, inherent style is the lifeboat the reader (soon-to-be listener) rides in. Don't think about adapting someone else's style or technique. Be yourself, but bigger!

√ Remember your audience

Trick: in your writing space, put up a picture of someone (or a handful of someones), real or imagined, that you're telling your story to (writing your masterpiece for). Establish rapport. Focus on telling your story to this person, and only this person.

√ Organization

"Writing is 90% organization and 10% actual writing."

Long-forgotten writer who was

exaggerating by about 50%

For new writers in particular, at the beginning there is a balancing act between your WRITING TIME and your need for ORGANIZATION. Organization is extremely important to the any creative artist, but critical for a writer. The way your desk is set up, the way you start and end your sessions, your approach to points, themes, stories, outlines, tense...depend on organization. See organization like building an airport. The more organized your writing, the easier it is for the creative devas and muses to land.

Bottom line: Until organization is a more natural part of your output, devote at least 10 MINUTES IN EACH WRITING SESSION to organizing your notes, your progress, your place in the process.

√ Who Are You Writing For?

Your speech may go through a number of drafts. The first draft is for you, and you only. Brainstorm. Brainstorm. Brainstorm. Don't worry about constraints of time, order or appropriateness. Write down all the main thoughts and ideas of your speech. Let the information and ideas for your message roll out of your mind and onto your paper or into your word processor). Forget about how long your speech might be. List everything you want your audience to know about your topic. Try to use complete sentences... but don't get goofy in the process. As regards this topic, you're the authority! Try to write at least l5 separate points.

There is no judgment, no critique, no editing in the first draft. This is you letting the material rear it's head. It's not at all about how it looks, how it's written, how it reads or what order it comes out in. You're sowing seeds. We can weed the garden later.

The second draft is for the audience. In this draft we get more into the

LISTENER'S HEAD. Now that you've communicated with yourself in the first draft, we want to connect with the audience. Here we pay more attention to style, tense, tension, etc.

The third draft is for results. Look through the eyes of your outcome and sharpen the edges, spice up the language, skim off the dross. In reality, the third draft is nothing more than a fine polish.

As you write your speech, stop and read aloud various sections of the material. Is it coming across? Does the order of your speech move from a strong introduction to a solid central core (with two to four main points, followed by supporting materials)? Is there an exciting conclusion?

√ Writer's Block

Many of us who write regularly, don't really think there is any such thing as Writer's Block. Instead we prefer to call it "The Ritual of Writing." Sometimes it flows, sometimes it doesn't. Calling it something other than Writer's Block shifts the power.

Tricks to take the power back:

1) Always complete your writing session. Finish in an organized manner. Finish sections and sub-sections, if possible. Be orderly. Write yourself a note detailing the exact nature of your progress: where you are in your writing, what you will work on now.

2) When really stuck, rewrite what you wrote in your last writing session. A page, a few paragraphs.

3) Tell the complete truth about what you're feeling when so-called Writer's Block shows up. Dig deeper. Express it.

4) Change something. Write in a different section, take a walk, change your clothes, take a shower, drink water, have a snack, dance.

5) If you're really stuck, don't try to write. Instead, on paper, interview yourself about your topic, ask probing, surprising

questions, or describe your emotional state.

√ The Zone

Like all creative endeavors, writing is about getting in the Zone. In the Zone, you're no longer doing the writing, the writing is just coming through you. The Zone is yours when you put your writing in the upper room in the pyramid. Be committed, Face the boogie man. You're on the cusp of true magic.

• Start With The Body

I know it seems sensible to just start writing the speech, first the opening, then the overview, then the body, etc. Don't do it. Start with the body, then go on to the opening and closing. The body is the "heart" of your message. Get clear on that first. You'll waste less time writing clever openings that don't fit your talk. Additionally, by working on the body first, you'll find out what's missing, what research needs to be done, what stories, anecdotes and illustrations you have to compile. You'll have more time to gather visuals.

"Mend your speech a little, lest it may mar your fortunes."

William Shakespeare

While writing the body, beware: most speakers try to tell us everything. You can't. Your audience doesn't want you to. They want to hear you on your subject because they assume you have ferreted out the less essential information and are bringing only the important, interesting points that can be shared in the allotted time. Plus, all audiences have limited attention spans. Period.

When in doubt, leave it out! You'll be our hero.

"Gentlemen, you have just been listening to that Chinese sage, On Too Long."

Will Rogers

Helpful hint: Use double space (or even triple space) when you write or type your material. This allows room for corrections and changes, and it makes it easier to learn your speech.

- Written Word vs. Spoken Word

Writing for a reader and writing for a listener are very different experiences. Written words and spoken words live in two separate worlds. Maybe you already know this. Some things that look fine on paper just don't sound right aloud. Conversely, some sections of your draft that may appear to be long-winded on paper sound perfectly natural and effective when read aloud.

A good speech writer needs to write for the ear. Most of us have learned to write for the eye, with no real regard for how the same sentences or phrases may sound said out loud. A few hints:

1) Use shorter, more down to-earth words.

"Last night, Japanese forces attacked Hong Kong.

This morning the Japanese attacked Midway Island."

FDR's declaration of war speech, December 8, 1941

A good example of short, to-the-point sentences

"Last night, your father said I looked fat.

This morning I put Exlax in his porridge."

Mom's declaration of war speech, March 22, 1967

A good example of short, to-the-point sentences

2) Be more concerned about communication than erudition. Use words that say what you mean, as opposed to using complicated, long or technical terms.

Turn your written words into a spoken message that you can deliver — comfortably and effectively, and to be consistently successful as a speaker or presenter, always say out loud anything you're going to say to a group of any kind.

•Short is Sweet

"Be brief, be sincere, be seated."

Franklin Delano Roosevelt

Focus your speech around one basic idea. Don't try to say everything, or your audience will retain zilch. Don't give an audience the whole meal. Give them a taste so they want to come back to the table. This is especially true for you folks who are speaking in order to get business from your audience. Finish while they still want to hear more.

"A storyful of sparkling wit will keep its audience grinning.

Especially if the end of it is close to the beginning."

Anonymous

Edit the hell out of your material. As I said, 100 words on paper convert to about a minute of speech time. Less is best. Limit the time for expounding on each point, especially so you can include audience participation.

Work backwards from your intended purpose. Ask yourself, "Does this story, this graphic, this fact or this example really help me make my point?" If you want your speech to be magic, saw the lady in half!

Chapter 18: Group Communication Jeopardy Styleheather Penn

Topic: Group Communication; A comprehensive Jeopardy game that focuses on vocabulary terms relating to group communication.

Learning Objectives: This learning activity is designed to:

Promote student engagement

Improve memorization skills

Improve content recall and understanding

Develop a community of learners

Correctly using the vocabulary words associated with group communications, students identify and define the key roles necessary for cohesive group function.

Engaging the students in play and friendly competition demands group compliance, reinforcing the roles and attributes learned in the classroom.

Description of Assignment/Activity: This activity is a form of the TV show Jeopardy. The teacher draws on the board a Jeopardy type board then fills in the numbers 100 – 500, five along the top and five down, totaling 25 numbered boxes (a PowerPoint can also be used). Each box corresponds with a question. If the correct answer is given the group gets the points. The game gradually gets harder as the points increase. Textbooks are allowed and encouraged as it ups the chances of a student digging and finding an answer. A second round is done in the same manner as the first. This rounds closure signifies a tallying of points and declaration of the winter. This is a good game for the middle of the semester when the students might start forgetting earlier terms.

Materials needed:

Notecards w/question & answer definitions on one side and a point amount on the other.

The textbook

Questions and answers

Prep time:

Five minutes drawing board or time required to create presentation

4 hours doing notecards

Assignment time: Depending on how hard the questions are and how knowledgeable a class is, the activity can take an hour to an hour and a half.

Instructions for Instructor:

The teacher draws a Jeopardy type grid on the board or uses a link online for an automated option or creates a PowerPoint. If writing on the board fill in the numbers 100 – 500, five along the top and five down, totaling 25 numbered boxes.

Based on the number of students in the class, break them up into 4 or 5 groups. There is no need to decide which team goes first as the group who answers the first question correctly earns that title.

Arrange notecards by point value on your desk to easily access.

Have them pick a box and ask the question from your notecards

If the answer is correct they may go again. There are two consecutive goes allowed then the turn is over. From the time the question is read the students have 30 seconds to give an answer if they don't another group can steal. A steal does not count as a consecutive turn.

The game carries on in much the same manner on into the second round called Double Jeopardy. Point value increases and questions get harder.

Categories may include, group roles, group norms and communication terms. A sample question may be: What is the term coined when a group focuses on inclusivity and doesn't seek outside sources or appoint a devil's advocate in group discussions or decisions? The answer: What is groupthink.

Instructions for Students:

Get into your assigned groups. Come up with a group name.

Look up at the board and select a category and point value marked on one of the 25 boxes. You will have 30 seconds to collaborate with your group to come up with an answer. Using the textbook is encouraged, just look fast you only have 30 seconds to answer once the question is given.

Answer the question correctly in the form of a question and win the and you go again (max. two consecutive). Fail to answer correctly and you lose your turn.

Help your group garner the most points to be crowned, winner. This could entail a prize. A prize may be no homework for the winning group.

Necessary Background: Jeopardy is a proper TV show; however, make sure your students have an understanding of the basic rules. Why does Jeopardy work in this context?

The group utilizes many of the skills being discussed in the text to collaborate, communicate and find the answers.

You should be able to get a feel for where your class is in understanding the material covered so far. Perhaps they were weaker in some areas and not others. You can cater the future teachings to encompass that deficit.

Variations: There are many ways this activity can be played. Instead of points, students can play for prizes, etc.

Trouble spots: There aren't many trouble spots with this activity. If the questions are too hard or to easy the game may run long or short. That can leave some unsatisfied.

Common Questions: Students usually ask about stealing the most.

Debrief: Ask the students to reflect on class strengths in terms of content knowledge and opportunities for improvement.

Chapter 19: 15 Tips That Will Help Transform You

So now, we have seen the benefits of a confident public speaker, and how this can boost your career; the qualities a great public speaker needs to have. We have analyzed a list of big names that have set examples in public speaking and a few names that have not been successful in the endeavor. We learnt from both the categories, taking away the skills we need to master and the mistakes to avoid.

Now we come to the last section of the book, where a list of actions point will give you a clear idea as to how to go about acquiring the skill sets and mastering them.

Preparation: A vital component to be confident in front of all those people is to absolutely ready with what you want to say. Spend a good amount of time and do your research thoroughly on the matter you will be speaking about. This will ensure that when you open the floor for question, you won't be nervous. Also when you are well read in the topic, in case you forget a part of your speech, you can easily improvise without fumbling.

Practice: No! Not memorize but practice. Mirrors can be great friends when you want to practice your presentation. It will give you an opportunity to rectify your posture, gestures and your body language as a whole especially now that you have watched videos of some excellent communicators.

Your Audience: It is absolutely necessary to research and understand your audience. You presentation needs to be able to cater rightly for your target audience otherwise you will lose them. Keep in mind the age group, sex, gender, religion and political orientation of the attendees, and create your presentation accordingly. You don't want bore the crowd with irrelevant stuffs or enrage them with a wrong statement.

Tools: One of the most effective and commonly used tools is the PowerPoint. It has become an integral part of a presentation where visual aids can wonders. It will keep the audience engaged, and fill in any gaps in understanding that a person might face from your words.

Environment: In order to look at home on stage and feel confident, try to visit the venue a day or two before the event. His will give you an opportunity to familiarize with the environment, and feel comfortable on the day of the presentation. Your ease and body language will keep the audience comfortable too.

Experience: Participate in as many opportunities as you are able to get in public speaking. With every presentation you will become better. Practice makes perfect, remember?

A Great Start: Yes, that's true. When your start the session in a great way, it will go a long way to keep your audience interested. The first impression you give them will set your image and make them curious. So begin with a little entertainment or something for them to smile about and you know you are off to a great presentation.

Engage Your Audience: If your audience has to listen to you for 30minutes or more, they might eventually become passive listeners. So why not give them some task to perform related to the topic of discuss. This will ensure that their interest level is maintained throughout the session and they have a better and stronger take away from the session.

Q & A: Try to reserve the last 15mins or so for questions. After informative or interesting session, the audience will definitely have questions for you. So don't simply give them an email id to contact you for questions, do the Q&A session live to make it more effective and interesting.

Dress Well: How you present yourself is as important as how you present your case. Remember that you as person will have to make a positive impression on the people watching you. Only then they will be interested in listening to what you have to say. Your dress should portray the role you are taking up.

Prompts: Do not write down you entire speech and take a huge paper to the stage. Use index cards to note down the major points which will give the order in which you have to discuss the topics and remind you if you miss out on any topic or point. This will help you flow through the session smoothly

Walk: Do not stand cemented to one corner of the stage or the center for that matter. Walk around the stage to make sure that your presence is felt by the audience listening to you. Walking around is a body language that emanates confidence and ease, a relaxed environment – all good attributes to consider. Also, walking will help drain the pent up excess energy that is causing the anxiety.

Constructive Feedback: Nothing better than getting constructive feedback and improving with every presentation you give. You can either include your friends, any family or your mentor or senior in the audience who would give you feedback and scope of improvements or you can distribute a feedback form to your audience to give you feedback from their point of view. Alternatively you can record each of your session and watch it later for self-reflection and provide yourself with feedback or give the video to someone you know can give you some constructive feedback.

Avoid fillers: Avoiding fillers like 'umm…' or 'ahh…' or 'so…' can be done by successful practice before the presentation. Fillers make you sound like you aren't sure of what you are going to say or that you have forgotten your speech. Fumbling and fillers are unattractive attributes of a public speaker.

Finish Well: Finishing it well is important as the last few words will stick to the mind of the people. Summarize and conclude well. Give them the key point they should be taking away from your session.

Chapter 20: Further Preparation

Here are more things to consider when getting ready to give your presentation. The first is to know your material as well as you possibly can. This means practice, practice, practice. Going over the speech again and again till you're totally confident it's the best you can do.

It means knowing the speech so well you don't have to read it. So why shouldn't you read it? The main reason is that you could be looking down at the paper much more than you do at your audience, which, in turn, means that you can't maintain eye contact with them. Thus you can't see how they're reacting because you're lost in your manuscript. And this does literally mean "lost" because it's easy to lose your place; lights often reflect in your eyes and prevent you seeing the material clearly. Since you're reading rather than speaking, the talk could sound mechanical.

What should you do then? First, do not, and I repeat, do not memorize the speech. If you do, you may be concentrating so hard on what comes next that again you pay little attention to your listeners. Also, what happens if you lose your train of thought, or in other words, forget what comes next?

What should you do then? You can use notes and not be tied to exact word or paragraphs. Rather, don't worry about whether the words are the same each time you practice. They shouldn't be. Rather, you should concentrate on the organization of the speech and on what you want to tell the audience than on what comes next. With notes you don't need to glance down so often. You can concentration more on the audience's reactions.

How should you rehearse? At first, go over your speech several times by yourself, enough times, in fact, that you feel confident. It can help to practice in front of a large mirror. It can also help if you record yourself and then judge how well you think you've done. But you don't have to do that because you can judge yourself by how you feel after you've gone over the speech. Do you feel good about it? Do you feel good but think you still need more practice. Once you have things down pat, ask a few people you trust to listen to the presentation.

This not only can help in correcting or improving things you might not even have been aware of, but it can give you more confidence that you'll do a good job. Do this—with different friends or family members—more than once if you feel the need.

Do as much as you can to build and maintain your confidence. A few years ago an actor was chosen as a cast member for a 1400-seat theatre. This was a summer stock theatre that drew large audiences. The actor was nervous, afraid he wouldn't do well. You know, of course, the kinds of feelings he had—the same that you experience at appearing in front of strangers. One night he walked out on stage, feeling nervous, as he had for the first few nights of the production. Suddenly, he had a thought, an epiphany. "If all these people in the audience, these people I'm afraid of, could do a better at this particular job at this particular time, they'd be the ones up here acting the part, and I'd be the one in the audience. After that all the negative nervousness and fear disappeared, and the man could concentrate on the audience and the role, not on himself.

Although this is a true story, nothing this "magical" might happen to you in one second to the next as it did with the actor, but he was right. He was the perfect choice for the role. If you've chosen your subject well and are fully informed about it, there should be no problem. You're the perfect one for your role as speaker at the particular time and place and for this particular topic.

Something else that can help is to project in your mind what's going to happen when you stand in front of the audience. Visualize yourself going through the speech. Visualize the joy of communicating, the joy of experiencing the audience's reaction. In other words, think positively about how things will go. By now you should feel confident that you'll do well. You won't be perfect, of course. No speaker is. But don't worry about the little things. If your words come out twisted, so what? It happens to everyone, yes, even in regular conversation. If you mispronounce a word, no big deal. Even if you drop your notes, it hardly matters. Most audiences are sympathetic...unless you're doing something deliberately to antagonize them. So the most they're going to feel is sympathy or empathy.

In a production of Arthur Miller's Death of a Salesman, during the scene where Linda is telling her sons that their father has been attempting to kill himself, it's at night and the three of them are sitting at the kitchen table. At one point Linda is to tighten the belt on her bathrobe, and stand up. During one night of the play's run, the woman playing Linda tightened her belt but accidentally caught the edge of the tablecloth inside it. When she stood, the table cloth, plus salt and pepper shakers and a sugar bowl crashed to the floor. But you know what? The audience was so engrossed in the scene, it was as if this hadn't even happened.

And if an audience can ignore something like that, you don't have to sweat the little things!

Using Slides and Other Visual Aids

Visual aids of various types help, particularly slides. A few things to remember about them, however: Don't use many because the audience won't remember most of them if you use a lot. Also make sure they are attractive and have sharp contrast so the audience can see them well. Vary the type of slides so that not all, for instance, contain text...which in itself may be hard to read.

Make sure the visual aids, whether slides of maps or drawings or charts, supplement what you say, not the other way around. Use them, of course, but don't allow them to overpower what you say.

Chapter 21: How To Organize And Assemble Your Presentation

Outline Your Points

After pinpointing the message of your presentation, you must determine how you will present it. A good way to prepare is to create an outline of the most important points you want to make throughout the presentation, and then add some brief scripting to help prompt you through a mind blank.

Get Your Points Together

Before you can create an outline, you need ideas and points to organize. To get the brain juices flowing, go through these three steps:

i. Determine which points support your message best and will help convey what you want your audience to know, understand, or feel.

ii. Determine a handful (three to five, in most cases) of the most important facts that seem the most relevant and necessary.

iii. Throw out anything that does not support those facts.

Gather Evidence

With your salient points in hand, flesh out each in detail. Think about how much support they may need through facts, figures, and other evidence. A presentation is just not credible enough without supporting materials. You could be as charming a speaker, but without evidence to back up your claims and show that what you say is true, no one will buy into it. Evidence provides the meat for what would otherwise be nothing but an outline of ideas.

Evidence brings the following to the table in a presentation:

i. Clarification: It elaborates on your ideas and/or position.

ii. Proof: It shows that what you say is true.

iii. Life: It makes your presentation more memorable and interesting.

A number of different types of evidence will work for your presentation. Here are a few to consider:

Facts and figures: Facts and figures refer to data verifiable by an outside source. These include:

i. Statistics:

Statistics is information explaining something in terms of size or frequency. Statistics may sound like facts, and figures, but they can be easily distorted, and manipulated to give an impression that they may not be true. Always consider the source of a statistic and what its agenda might be. It is best to seek out multiple sources and their statistics to make sure the one you want to use is accurate. Also, be sure to use only current information because statistics can often get out of date quickly.

ii. Statements by authorities:

Statements from authorities refer to quotes from people with proven expert knowledge in a particular field of learning. Sometimes, popular figures such as politicians, television, or radio personalities, academicians etc. are worth quoting, but unless they are speaking to their profession, they should not be presented as authorities. When quoting experts that are not well known, you may need to mention their credentials in order to lend credence to the quote.

iii. Testimony:

Testimonies are supporting statements by others. There are three general types of testimony:

· Expert testimony: Same as statements by authority mentioned previously.

· Prestige testimony: Popular figures such as politicians, business personalities, or movie stars.

· Lay testimony: A civilian who is not necessarily an expert on the subject but can shed some light on it. This type of testimony is usually used to show that a problem or issue exists and may even be prevalent.

iv. Narratives:

Narratives are stories that illustrate a point by triggering the imagination through imagery. Similar to your presentation, narratives should have a beginning, middle, and end. They should also be pertinent and free of too many unnecessary tangents and other details. The human mind hasn't changed much since ancient people spread information through myths and epic poetry therefore stories still pass information more effectively than most other forms of communication.

v. Definitions:

A definition is a brief precise statement of what a word or an expression means, and sometimes the usage of the word or expression such as is found in a dictionary. You have three different types of definitions at your disposal:

· Dictionary: The standard meaning that comes from the dictionary.

· Etymological: The history of a word's development and where it came from.

· Operational: A measurement for a concept or idea that eludes easy definition. For example, happiness, which can be defined many ways, could be defined in one particular situation as the number of times someone smiles.

vi. Humour:

Funny stories related to the topic may get attention and ease the crowd, but sometimes they just may not be appropriate.

Mix and Match Types of Evidence

Of these evidence types, only facts and figures, statistics, and testimony can actually prove anything. If you really want to prove something, you will need to include one or more of them in your presentation to strengthen your argument. Additionally, you may want to also include other types of evidence as well, such as a narrative or two to show the subject in human terms, or humour to ease the crowd. Combining evidence both builds an effective argument and keeps your listeners engaged.

Select an Organizational Structure

The next trick after gathering your information is to organize it. The body of your presentation needs some kind of order; otherwise, you will end up like one of those unfortunate speakers who jump from one subject to another seemingly at random, repeating things and never getting to the point. Stick to an organizational structure and you can avoid those problems.

How you organize depends on your overall topic. Certain subjects lend themselves naturally to certain structures, the most common of which are:

· Topical: Relates distinct ideas to the theme and makes each a main point. Most useful for informative speeches.

· Chronological: Framed around a time sequence or logical progression. Useful for both informative and persuasive speeches because each requires background information.

- Classification: Puts material into categories. Useful for both informative and persuasive speeches.

- Problem/Solution: Describes a problem and presents a solution. Most useful for persuasive speeches.

- Cause/Effect: Describes the cause of a problem and then presents its effects. Most useful for persuasive speeches.

One of these patterns will work for most subjects, but it has to support your message and the goal of the presentation. Whichever way you choose, just make sure you stick with it throughout the presentation because, jumping from one organization plan to another can be almost as confusing as having no organization plan at all. As you are organizing, consider which materials will go with each point and which will bring your evidence to life.

Transitions

How you move from your presentation's introduction to its main body, from point to point within the main body, and from there to the conclusion, can make or break you as a presenter. That is why transitions are so important.

Transition statements move your audience from one idea to the next. In one or two sentences, they wrap up your last idea and move it into your next idea. If handled properly, transition statements can make your presentation all the more smooth, polished, and engaging to a crowd.

Transitions make the presentation go round. Think of transitions as the cement that bonds together the structure of your presentation. They help your audience from getting confused as they absorb the information you provide. If your points had no markers between them and ran together with no distinction, listeners might not realize that you have moved on to a new topic or why the current evidence you are providing is relevant.

The audience will eventually figure it out, but that will take precious time in which they will not listen to you as closely, possibly missing some of your presentation. Even worse, they may blame you for gumming things up, which will cost you credibility. Audiences may not notice the transitions in a presentation, but they will definitely notice those that they are missing.

Well-crafted transitions come in two flavours:

i. The kind that reinforces your speech's organization:

This approach emphasizes where your presentation has been and where it is headed, letting the audience know that you've finished point A and are moving on to point B, so it is time to switch gears and prepare for new information.

ii. The kind that demonstrates how your ideas relate to the theme of your presentation:

This method pulls the listeners back for a moment to remind them of the main topic that brought them to your presentation in the first place before further elaborating on it.

There is only a fine line of difference between these two approaches, and both can be mixed and matched interchangeably. In fact, the best transitions perform both of these functions.

Give your transitions a trial run. Although you should never completely script a presentation, you should always at least plan your transitions ahead of time. Transitions are the easiest elements of a presentation to forget, especially if you are nervous and just want to get your time in front of the crowd over with. Practicing transitions ahead of time ensures you will not forget them later.

Conclusion

Now that you have read this book, you have the tools you need to greatly improve your performance when public speaking, as well as reducing the stress and anxiety of such events. While all of these tools are beneficial you don't have to use them all in order to achieve success. Instead, find those that resonate with you and prove more compatible with your personality and skill sets.

As mentioned throughout, the most important thing is to be true to yourself when giving a public presentation. Therefore, apply the methods in this book that help you to be more natural, comfortable and confident in your efforts. The very best of luck to you and your journey into successful public speaking!